Lecture Notes in Computer Science 10152

Commenced Publication in 1973
Founding and Former Series Editors:
Gerhard Goos, Juris Hartmanis, and Jan van Leeuwen

Editorial Board

More information about this series at http://www.springer.com/series/7407

Sergiy Bogomolov · Matthieu Martel
Pavithra Prabhakar (Eds.)

Numerical Software Verification

9th International Workshop, NSV 2016
Toronto, ON, Canada, July 17–18, 2016
Revised Selected Papers

 Springer

Editors
Sergiy Bogomolov
IST Austria
Klosterneuburg
Austria

Matthieu Martel
Université de Perpignan
Perpignan
France

Pavithra Prabhakar
Kansas State University
Manhattan, KS
USA

ISSN 0302-9743   ISSN 1611-3349 (electronic)
Lecture Notes in Computer Science
ISBN 978-3-319-54291-1   ISBN 978-3-319-54292-8 (eBook)
DOI 10.1007/978-3-319-54292-8

Library of Congress Control Number: 2017932122

LNCS Sublibrary: SL1 – Theoretical Computer Science and General Issues

Printed on acid-free paper

This Springer imprint is published by Springer Nature
The registered company is Springer International Publishing AG
The registered company address is: Gewerbestrasse 11, 6330 Cham, Switzerland

Preface

The articles contained in this volume were presented at the 9th International Workshop on Numerical Software Verification (NSV), held during July 17–18, 2016, in Toronto, Ontario, Canada. The NSV workshop is alternatively collocated with the International Conference on Computer Aided Verification (CAV) and the Cyber-Physical Systems Week (CPSWeek). In 2016, NSV was organized jointly with the 28th International Conference on Computer Aided Verification.

Numerical computations are ubiquitous in digital systems: supervision, prediction, simulation, and signal processing rely heavily on numerical calculus to achieve desired goals. The design and verification of numerical algorithms have a unique set of challenges, which set it apart from rest of software verification. To achieve the verification and validation of global properties, numerical techniques need to precisely represent the local behaviors of each component. The implementation of numerical techniques on modern hardware adds another layer of approximation because of the use of finite representations of infinite precision numbers that usually lack basic arithmetic properties such as commutativity and associativity. Finally, the development and analysis of cyber-physical systems that involve the interacting continuous and discrete components pose a further challenge. It is hence imperative to develop logical and mathematical techniques for reasoning about programmability and reliability. The NSV workshop is dedicated to the development of such techniques.

The papers of the edition were reviewed by the Program Committee, whose help is gratefully acknowledged. The invited speakers at NSV 2016 were Alessandro Abate (University of Oxford, UK), Thomas Heinz (Robert Bosch GmbH, Germany), Eric Feron (Georgia Institute of Technology, USA), Behzad Samadi (Maplesoft, Waterloo, Ontario, Canada), Yassamine Seladji (University of Tlem- cen, Algeria), and Cesare Tinelli (University of Iowa, USA).

The first eight NSV meetings were held in Princeton, New Jersey, collocated with CAV (2008), San Francisco, California, collocated with CPSWeek (2009), Edinburgh, UK, collocated with FLoC (2010), Salt Lake City, Utah, collocated with CAV (2011), Berkeley, California, collocated with CAV (2012), Philadelphia, Pennsylvania, collocated with CPSWeek (2013), Vienna, Austria, collocated with CAV (2014), and Seattle, Washington, collocated with CPSWeek (2015).

December 2016

Sergiy Bogomolov
Matthieu Martel
Pavithra Prabhakar

Organization

Program Chairs

Sergiy Bogomolov	Institute of Science and Technology Austria, Austria
Matthieu Martel	Université de Perpignan, France
Pavithra Prabhakar	Kansas State University, USA

Program Committee

Stanley Bak	Air Force Research Lab, Rome, USA
Ezio Bartocci	Vienna University of Technology, Austria
Sylvie Boldo	Inria, France
Olivier Bouissou	CEA, France
Alexandre Chapoutot	ENSTA ParisTech, France
Nasrine Damouche	Université de Perpignan, France
Georgios Fainekos	Arizona State University, USA
Mirco Giacobbe	Institute of Science and Technology Austria, Austria
Eric Goubault	CEA, France
Susmit Jha	University of California, Berkeley, USA
James Kapinski	Toyota, USA
Ian Mitchell	University of British Columbia, Canada
Dejan Nickovic	Austrian Institute of Technology, Austria
Corina Pasareanu	NASA Ames Research Center, USA
Oleg Sokolsky	University of Pennsylvania, USA
Walid Taha	Halmstad University, Sweden and Rice University, USA
Mahesh Viswanathan	University of Illinois at Urbana-Champaign, USA

Contents

Verification of Networks of Smart Energy Systems over the Cloud

Alessandro Abate[✉]

Department of Computer Science, University of Oxford, Oxford, UK
aabate@cs.ox.ac.uk

Abstract. This contribution advocates the use of formal methods to verify and certifiably control the behaviour of computational devices interacting over a shared infrastructure. Formal techniques can provide compelling solutions not only when safety-critical goals are the target, but also to tackle verification and synthesis problems on populations of such devices: we argue that alternative solutions based on classical analytical techniques or on approximate computations are prone to errors with global repercussions, and instead propose an approach based on formal abstractions, error-based refinements, and the use of interface functions for the synthesis of abstract controllers and their concrete implementation. Two applicative areas are elucidated, dealing respectively with thermal loads and electricity-generating devices interacting over a smart energy network or over a local power grid. We discuss the aggregation of large populations of thermostatically-controlled loads and of photovoltaic panels, and the corresponding problems of energy management in smart buildings, of demand-response on smart grids, and respectively of frequency stabilisation and grid robustness.

Keywords: Cyber-physical systems · Systems of systems · Internet of things · Hybrid models · Stochastic processes · Nondeterminism · Partial observations · Real-time systems · Security · Model learning · (quantitative) probabilistic verification · Formal abstractions · Bisimulations · Statistical verification · Feedback controllers · Policy and strategy synthesis · Distributed control · Safety and performance · Games · Correct-by design synthesis · Autonomy · Energy and power networks · Electricity demand-response · Thermostatically controlled loads · Smart buildings and smart grids · Photovoltaic panels · Blackouts · Aggregations of large populations

1 Technological Context: Networks of Complex Systems

There is an ever increasing trend to place and integrate computational devices over the cloud. By "cloud" we denote an infrastructure (predominantly with digital features over physical qualities) allowing for seamless (mostly wireless) communication between devices, which thus give form to a network of distinct

© Springer International Publishing AG 2017
S. Bogomolov et al. (Eds.): NSV 2016, LNCS 10152, pp. 1–14, 2017.
DOI: 10.1007/978-3-319-54292-8_1

components[1]. Such devices are nowadays identified as "smart" – this attribute denotes a capability to engage with the environment (over the cloud) that is not purely static: indeed modern devices are clearly changing from having reactive features to active ones; not only do they interact passively with the environment (neighbouring devices, or a population-level feedback from the whole network), but also internally learn from it and indeed actively engage with it by modifying it locally. This interaction, which is either digital or physical depending on the type of interconnection or embedding within the medium, leads to repercussions over adjacent devices. As such, unlike static or purely reactive elements, these devices comprise internal dynamics that are locally actively coupled with neighbouring components.

Such devices are furthermore often "complex", in that they encompass both digital components and (possibly) analogue ones, and are likely to evolve (internally, or spatially within their environment) according to non-trivial dynamics. Digital components may comprise the computational platforms they run on, or the logic-based control architectures that affect their dynamical behaviour, whereas analogue parts may encompass the physical medium they are embedded into, or the continuous components making up the devices themselves.

These devices is often referred to as "cyber-physical systems" (CPS), and the network they are part of is thought of as a "system of systems" (SOS), or as "internet of things" (IoT). The first acronyms seem to be more relevant within engineering contexts, whereas the second depicts a more abstract concept (it does not necessarily distinguish between digital and analogue components, nor automatically emphasises the networking or dynamical aspects) and appears in use within the applied mathematics literature. The third and last seems to be widespread within the computer sciences and in general involves fewer elements of coordination, actuation, and dynamics than CPS.

We are thus facing an engineering platform of multiple, interleaving and interacting complex systems, a true "system of systems" with issues of synchronisation and coordination, feedback from couplings and interactions, and with a global behaviour that is emergent from local dynamics. Such complex systems are thus not monolithic, and entail issues of operational independence, geographical distribution and heterogeneity, and local adaptability. We argue throughout this work that this network ought to be quantitatively analysed, by means of formal methods that are based on mathematical models of the single system components and of their networked interactions. Beyond analysis, autonomy can be established by means of modern feedback control architectures, which ought to be certified and indeed be "correct-by-design".

It is often the case that such complex systems are only partially known, that is they are not exactly nor fully observed, and possibly subject to uncertainty and/or randomness. We intend the latter aspect to be due to the presence of heterogeneity, noise, random or chaotic (and as such not precisely predictable) behaviours (as with, say, weather forecast), or to the presence of human users in

---

[1] In this context we do not distinguish between computations performed over the cloud (fog computing) or the edge of this platform.

the loop (interfering with - or perhaps supporting - the autonomy aspects of the system). All such elements are in general hard to model deterministically, but can be encompassed by probabilistic terms (whether objectively or subjectively construed). Notice that we distinguish this presence (probability) from that of environmental non-determinism (to be separately discussed in each of the next parts). These assumptions lead to the consideration of stochastic behaviours in the systems under study, either at the level of their dynamics (this is known as process noise), or upon their observations (e.g., sensors uncertainty or noise).

We take this opportunity to clarify and distinguish among two different aspects, both relevant but distinct to the systems under consideration. On the one hand, this setup deals with issues of learning within the single devices comprising the overall CPS. Learning can be directed towards models of the devices, as well as towards specifications (harvesting requirements). On the other hand, the platform comprises issues of computation, communication, and control. Whilst learning issues are data-based, and require bottom-up studies, the latter set of problems naturally require top-down analysis and are classically model-based. The first issue (learning) is internal to the device interacting (via sensing and actuation) with and adapting to the local environment. The second issue (communication) deals with the specifics of the processing and exchange of information within and among devices.

Next, we move from the perspective of the practical engineering setups, to that of their mathematical models. This new perspective allows for the development of quantitative analysis tools, and to obtain results leveraging the area of formal methods.

2   Formal Verification of Complex Models

Quantitative issues such as reliability, safety, dependability, are key in practical applications of the complex engineering setups that we have previously introduced. These issues play a central role either because the components belong to safety-critical applications, or because it is often the case that the complex network of systems is comprised within a safety-critical setup: much like existing complex engineering infrastructures, in an era of increasing inter-connectivity systems are seldom isolated, thus safety criticality depends on coupled behaviours and thus represents a global network issue.

The need for formal methods is therefore key. The use of these techniques is an alternative to approaches based on qualitative analysis, relying on more classical mathematics and often focusing on global, network-level properties, which are seldom useful in a complex context preventing analytical or explicit mathematical results. The use of formal methods is further in juxtaposition to fine-grained agent-based modelling and related simulation-based techniques, or to statistical approaches, which are known to be stymied with a number of limitations: they establish presence of potential faults or errors, but cannot assert their absence in general; they hardly scale when non-determinism and stochasticity play a relevant role in the dynamics, and when the system under study presents continuous (uncountable) variables interleaved with discrete components (discontinuous). Sample-based techniques further lack formal guarantees, which is in particular a fundamental limitation when single devices or whole systems are to be certified (as opposed to be validated towards quality assurance). On the other hand these approaches should not be completely dismissed, but rather integrated within the use of formal approaches which, as is known, present computational limitations when applied to large-scale and complex models, as is the case of the engineering setups under study.

Formal verification techniques hinge on quantitative models. The verification of quantitative models of complex systems requires handling a mathematical formalism encompassing dynamical variables evolving over hybrid (continuous/discrete) state spaces, comprising probabilistic behaviours, possibly with continuous-time semantics, and under partial observations of the model's variables. Emerging from a broad research initiative on alternative models of computation, a natural modelling framework encompassing all these aspects is that of stochastic hybrid models [5]. Such models are dynamically rich and require modern, tailored techniques for analysis, verification and synthesis.

At the outset, it is easy to realise that the verification of such models is bound to undecidability results, unless the problem at hand admits an analytical (that is, explicit) solutions, which is quite unlikely in view of models complexity and of the possibly rich objectives under consideration [18]. On the other hand, state-of-the-art software tools for automated quantitative model checking of complex models (e.g., the PRISM model checker) are not applicable to models comprising all the aspects discussed above. As a partial attainment of the grand goal of verification of truly complex models, literature has seen probabilistic model checking of finite-state models, model checking of concurrent models with continuous (dense) time semantics, reachability-based verification of (non-probabilistic) hybrid dynamical models, and some timid early attempts to provide partial evaluation of more complex models – all daunted by the sheer complexity of the goal. Notice that the mentioned successful verification instances apply to strict subsets of the target models of interest that have been discussed previously.

This body of work has been extended to deal with the verification of non-deterministic models – such extensions are often bound to conservative outcomes (whenever non-determinism in quantified universally), or to rather different synthesis frameworks (whenever non-determinism in quantified universally). The application of SAT or SMT techniques can be of particular interest for this goal, as well as results on robustness analysis, as classically investigated in control theory or, more recently, in formal methods.

If formal verification tools have not been fully extended and thoroughly applied to complex models, might complex models be compelled to fit existing formal methods tools? The next section elaborates on this goal.

The wider accessibility properties and interconnectivity features that modern smart devices allow carry as a drawback increased pressure towards issues of security. Security deals with coping with interferences of various sorts and nature, often thrusted in surreptitious and hidden manner, which can affect the correct functioning of the single devices and can potentially lead to global repercussions. Amongst major categories of cyber security threats we (non comprehensively) list those affecting resilience and privacy, as well as malicious intrusions and attacks. Notice that the presence of security attacks requires models semantics that are fundamentally different than those (non-deterministic or probabilistic) used to describe the presence of the environment. In this security context, various frameworks have been put forward: from worst-case non-deterministic approaches, to average-case probabilistic models, to (possibly stochastic) game-theoretical frameworks. Of them, the latter approach appears to encompass the nature of potential attacks and of possible replies, mitigations, or preventions actions against them.

Key aspects at the interface of communication and computation are those dealing with real-time engineering. These, within a networking perspective, relate to important computational issues of inter-operability, synchronisation, and concurrency; and, from the communications perspective, to problems of network theory and issues of data integration within models.

Whilst understood as key in the context of CPS applications, we do not delve into details of such problems any further in this essay.

3 Approximate Model Checking of Stochastic and Hybrid Models

This contribution is underpinned by recent research on stochastic hybrid models [5]. Properties of interest are usually encoded within known and exploited modal logics, such as PCTL or CSL (whether in continuous or discrete time), or just by looking at the likelihood attached to trajectories verifying linear time specifications expressed in LTL or as (e.g., Büchi) automata over infinite strings. Extensions to conditional probabilities have been pursued in recent literature.

Over related frameworks of stochastic and hybrid models, a number of authors have recently investigated the characterisation of basic probabilistic reachability and invariance specifications [5], as well as the extension to reach-avoid (constrained reachability), and to richer properties such as linear-time properties expressed as a DFA or as Büchi automata [19]. With regards to the latter, infinite-horizon properties have been also studied, and involve advanced analytical tools [18].

Beyond characterisation and towards numerical assessment, the properties above have been computed by means of finite abstractions [3, 4]. The derivation of formal errors due to such finite abstractions [9] has effectively led to the development of approximate model checking of stochastic hybrid models. Errors have been further extended and refined [12, 19], and embedded in the development of a software tool, which feeds complex models to probabilistic model checking software packages.

FAUST^2 [13] is a Matlab-based software tool, which accepts as an input a stochastic process and a formal specification, and generates a finite abstraction that can be fed into a probabilistic model checker such as PRISM or MRMC.

The abstraction is guaranteed to abide by a user-defined error that is required on the satisfaction of the given property of interest. The error is computed based on the underlying dynamics of the SHS and on the given property [9], and encompasses the difference between the probability distributions (in time) of concrete and abstract models. It has been shown that such error induces an approximate probabilistic bisimulation relation between the concrete and the (finite) abstract models [1,15], which can be also of use to study transient dynamical properties [2,11,17]. The overall procedure leads to an anytime algorithm, which sequentially refines coarse model abstractions, based on an update of the computed bound on the current error [9].

Related results have been developed by approximating the concrete stochastic model with a noiseless abstraction [20,22], which is then deterministically verified by means of software tools for dynamical models, such as PESSOA. The outcome allows for the refinement of assertions or of synthesised controllers, in view of a quantified error of the abstraction procedure. Unlike the approach described earlier, the new error encompasses (a moment of) the absolute value of the difference between the solutions of the two models, and is shown to exist under certain contractivity (which is a form of stability) assumptions on the concrete model dynamics.

Cognate research on verification of stochastic (and hybrid) dynamical models has been looking at the use of stochastic SAT modulo theory, the recasting of a verification objective as the solution of a PDE (with associated numerics), or the approximation of the above quantitative verification problems as convex optimisation ones.

The lack of full access to the state variables leads to the setup of partially observed modes, of which a known instance is that of hidden Markov models. In view of undecidability issues, substantial work on heuristics for the analysis of these models within the field of artificial intelligence. Formally, this setup requires the introduction of sufficient statistics and work over a belief space which, with the exception of linear models with additive Gaussian noise and associated corresponding Kalman estimators, is in general prone to lack analytical and computational tractability. Further work, both theoretical and algorithmic, is most definitely needed on this class of models.

The verification of parametric models encompassing non-determinism has not been focus of thorough and practically scalable investigation, regardless of whether seen as internal (to be universally quantified against) or external (to be synthesised over). Perhaps further steps can be attained by principled use of SMT approaches, or of results in robustness analysis.

A known and evident concern on the applicability of model-based quantitative verification techniques is the issue of scalability: these approaches are known to be stymied by state-space explosion, which is particularly relevant for complex CPS models. It is necessary to mitigate this issue by means of a multi-pronged approach: exploiting model modularity and topological distributivity, use of assume-guarantee reasoning, employment of deep compositional results, interfacing with legacy systems (and corresponding models), use of paradigms of object-oriented programming, and development of state-less abstractions [21]. On the other hand, it is well understood that sample-based techniques (such as in paradigms of runtime verification and testing) have the potential to scale to complex models, whilst on the down side they suffer from lack of tight performance guarantees. Within the context of formal verification, it is then of utmost interest to provide a novel formal integration of sample-based techniques within model-based deductive approaches [14]. As a side comment, learning algorithms can be directed towards models of the devices, as well as towards specifications (harvesting requirements). Towards this direction, the employment of coverage metrics has recently grown much interest.

As much as sample-based techniques or agent-based simulations seldom provide formal performance guarantees, approaches based on (non-formal) approximate computations are stymied by lack of certified behaviour. For instance, employing continuous mean-field limits (which are shown correct exclusively at asymptotic limits) renders an intrinsically probabilistic population a deterministic problem, which prevents the generation of certain allowable fringe behaviours. Further, the use of grid-based techniques with no control of the precision is bound to lead to suboptimal solutions, or errors that accumulate fast with time and which certainly do not meet any certification requirement or formal guarantee.

In conclusion, we argue that model verification based on classical analytical techniques has shown its limits, whereas sample-based results or outcomes based on non-formal approximate computations are prone to generate uncontrollable errors with overreaching global repercussions. We argue that a principled application of formal methods techniques, properly enhanced via computationally-prone approaches, is the way forward particularly for CPS applications.

4 From Verification to Synthesis: Correct-by-Design Control of Complex Models

Beyond quantitative verification, control synthesis also requires proper formalisation over complex models. As discussed, control is a form of external non-determinism, and as such it has to be contrasted with forms of non-determinism that are resolved by the environment, that are due to coarse-grained abstractions (internal non-determinism), or with (static) parametric uncertainty. The semantics of external non-determinism involve a volitive agent, which selects functions of time and of the state, possibly in a randomised manner and accounting for past history. Such selection leads to control laws known as policies or strategies. It is often of interest to focus on memoryless laws, possibly deterministic ones, which limit the computational overhead and do not infringe the Markov property of the closed-loop model. Classical control synthesis deals with performance criteria (introduced either as costs or rewards that are function of the state and/or the action space), over which optimality is sought via (respectively) minimisation or maximisation on a finite- or infinite-time horizon, within a predefined class of allowable policies. Of course such an approach can be applied to the goal of maximising the likelihood of verifying a quantitative property, such as those in PCTL logics discussed above for stochastic processes. The study of finite-horizon quantitative properties expressed in PCTL boils down to a characterisation via multiplicative cost functions [5], whereas that of infinite-horizon properties can be reduced to reachability computation over a product automaton [19]. The study of infinite horizon reachability is tricky since it involves extended notions of absorbing sets that are related to classical ones of bottom strongly connected components, or of max-end components [18]. Even more so in the case of controller synthesis over infinite-horizon properties [19].

Of course it is of interest to expand the issue of synthesis over both quantitative specifications and over performance: this can be done by resorting to techniques for multi-criteria or lexicographic optimisation. This goal has been recently pursued both within the computer science area, the control theory, and the optimisation literature.

Beyond process noise affecting the state dynamics, lack of exact observations (as partial access to the hidden variables or presence of sensor noise) lead to partially observed models, such as POMDP. As in the previous section, control synthesis for partially observable models brings along a number of technical and computational hurdles which, whilst thoroughly investigated within artificial intelligence and control literature, have only in part led to results that can be deemed satisfactory within the stricter context of formal methods.

Control synthesis problems are further prone to be extended to stochastic (two-and-a-half player) games [8]. Games can be played against the environment (e.g., towards compositional reasoning) or against an adversary (e.g., for applications in security). The author recognises interesting connections between game-theoretical setups in applied mathematics and control theory (for instance, dealing with existential results over uncountable models) and problems that are algorithmically solved for discrete configurations in theoretical computer science. The concept of formal abstractions (discussed in the previous section) could provide a link between results in the two areas.

The digital platform that characterises networks of complex systems, which we called "cloud" earlier, encompasses pervasive elements of wireless communications, and moves away from older, tethered communications, thus allowing for more agile reconfigurations as well as practical mobility of the agents in the network. As much as general communication aspects (real-time issues, protocol design aspects, and the like) need to be dealt with at the level of modelling, the specific deployment of wireless channels require proper handling of packets corruption or losses, and delays. Accepting that controllers are not necessarily embedded in a monolithic plant, but rather separated from it by a communication network, a recent and lively literature [23] has started to investigate issues of communication within control theoretical architectures.

As much as verification algorithms applied to complex CPS models suffer from state-space explosion, control synthesis ones are stymied by Bellman's curse of dimensionality. Techniques aimed at speeding up such formal algorithms (either via abstractions, or via approximations, or through compositionality, or also by mans of data-driven approaches, such as reinforcement learning) are naturally seen of much priority in this area.

5   Verification of Networks of Smart Energy Systems over the Cloud

In this section we provide a compelling application of the concepts, models and problems elaborated above. We discuss how present-day energy networks and electricity grids are transitioning to become interconnected networks of complex and smart systems, dynamically coupled both physically and over the cloud. We argue that their formal verification and correct-by-design control is relevant in engineering and industrial contexts, as well as for the market opportunities that they have the potential to catalyse. We provide two case studies zooming in on, respectively, the smart grid (investigated from the perspective of smart buildings in [6]) and electricity networks (elaborated in the project [7]).

Smart Buildings over the Smart Grid. Buildings consume more than 40 % of the energy in Europe. In order to sustainably reduce energy consumption by improving their usage and management, an optimal operation and an improved commissioning and maintenance of building management systems (BMS) are seen as key factors by the sector's industry. Efficient automation systems embedded in so-called "smart buildings" can indeed reduce the energy consumption up to an estimated thirty percent in many relevant instances. The objective of a smart building is to deliver useful building services that make occupants comfortable and productive (for instance, providing regulation for thermal comfort and air quality), at the lowest energy costs, over the entire building life cycle. This objective requires adding intelligence to the infrastructure of buildings and utilising information technology during their operation. This enables the connectivity of devices and components in a building (think of home automation devices, smart appliances, an application related to the broad area known as the "Internet of Things"), the interaction of buildings with their occupants and building operators or with their building management systems, as well as (at a higher level) their connection to other buildings or infrastructure components within a smart grid platform.

Such modern features and capabilities have opened new challenges related to the optimised performance of smart buildings, as (components of) networks of complex dynamical systems. Indeed, both the interconnection of smart BMS devices (such as sensorised HVAC modules) within a smart building, and (at a higher level) the local interaction of various buildings within a smart grid, clearly lead to the CPS configurations discussed above.

In the context of a single building, the construction of models that accurately capture the time evolution of its physical variables can be based on data gathered from the buildings. The continuous nature of physical variables, the discrete feature of digital controllers, and the presence of uncertainty originating from the environment and from the users behaviour, render the general framework of

Stochastic Hybrid Systems well-suited for modelling purposes [5]. Formal models enable the solution of engineering problems, such as optimal temperature regulation in a building, which in view of the slow dynamics we argue can be promising to tackle in the loop via formal methods. The stochastic and time-varying nature of the system under study suggests that a data-based update of the model, and more generally an integration of on-line data within the models under study [14], are of interest.

At a higher level, each building can be thought as a node in a network, such as a smart grid, partaking alongside other energy-consuming buildings in its dynamics, as well as interacting with devices generating energy. The connection with the CPS framework is again evident. Due to their flexibility in providing services to occupants, smart buildings can then be engaged in services by energy companies, such as load shifting, peak shaving, and more general in demand-response programs. As a result, whilst we can naturally think of engineering problems such as robustness and resiliency of the energy dynamics within a local smart grid, there is another layer of problems dealing with market design for demand response, with the engagement of consumers over grid markets, such as the electricity one (related to load shifting and consumers' demand response) and that dealing with economy of energy production (as per the concept of prosumers) and storage (zero net-energy buildings).

Within these CPS configurations, it is important to understand how global dynamics emerge from single dynamics and local interactions. One way to look at global dynamics arising from local contributions is to develop aggregation techniques: model aggregations lump together the dynamics of single buildings, providing a global description that is computable and scales well with the size of the problem.

Recent research has developed a procedure based on formal abstractions [10], which generates a finite stochastic dynamical model as an aggregation of the continuous temperature dynamics of a (possibly heterogeneous) population of Thermostatically Controlled Loads (TCL), which are basic models for the dynamics in smart buildings. The temperature of each single TCL is described by a stochastic difference equation and the TCL status by a deterministic switching mechanism – in all, a hybrid model. The procedure is formal as it allows the exact quantification of the error introduced by the abstraction. Research has discussed extensions to the case of controlled TCL, with dynamics affected by an aggregator (which could be a utility company engaged with consumers on demand response schemes). The structure of a control scheme (centralised, decentralised or distributed) hinges on many assumptions on the placement of sensors and on the capability of the actuators (HVAC modules), and in general on the information flow between the central aggregator and the single components of the population. The employment of distributed architectures appears to be relevant to optimise both engineering and economic goals.

We argue that approaches based on formal aggregation can be relevant both at an engineering level (working out precise approaches for safe and optimised energy consumption in a building, or for reliable and robust operation of a smart grid) as well as at a financial level (understanding fairness in market design between energy providers and customers over demand response schemes [16]). In conjunction with the development of formal models and quantitative verification approaches, abstractions can offer a principled approach to the understanding of the complex dynamics of smart buildings, and to their optimised and certifiable operation within the context of smart grids.

Renewables Generation over the Power Grid. The previous section has suggested how the engagement of consumers over a smart grid had the potential to lead to some paradigm shifts: from a centralised and fuel-based grid operation to a decentralised and renewable-based economy; from passive electricity and gas consumers supplied by energy utility companies, to active electricity prosumers and as such to utility companies partners (if not competitors). The grid becomes an accessible infrastructure to be locally leveraged in both directions by numerous players on the energy market.

Smart buildings have the capability to generate energy by means of renewables, as is the case of photovoltaic panels or wind turbines. In many regions worldwide, renewables are increasingly relied upon for electricity generation. As much as beneficial green energy can be regarded towards a sustainable decrease of greenhouse gases, the de-carbonisation of energy usage, and the long-term goal of zero net-energy buildings, renewables pose challenging engineering problems in view of their distributed engagement within a power grid that was conceived and built for centralised production and distribution, and of the intrinsically volatile quality of the electricity generated, which hinges on meteorological and local grid conditions. The decentralised nature of energy generation and its close connection with its distribution clearly suggest the presence of features of a network of complex systems, with evident CPS modelling opportunities.

Transmission System Operators (TSO) have to ensure the physical balancing of the power grid (the total electricity generation must match the total electricity consumption). In AC electrical grids, the frequency (50 Hz in nominal conditions) indicates whether or not the system is balanced. More and more Photo-Voltaic (PV) Panels are installed in distribution grids and they are not directly controllable by the TSO (unless organised in structured, large PV farms). In order to assess the safe operation and robustness of the whole system, TSO ought to take PV panels dynamical behaviours into account.

Recent research has attempted to formalise and implement a formal study of large populations of PV Panels. We have focused on the modelling of the dynamics of PV panels and their interaction with the power grid as Markov models. Within the broad goal of formal aggregation of large-scale populations of Markov models, and the objective to provide new computational algorithms for the optimal policy synthesis over such a population, we have looked at aggregating and controlling large populations of photovoltaic panels over the power grid.

We plan to again employ techniques from formal methods to generate quantitative abstractions of models of interest (large populations of PV panels), with specific predictive capabilities and a guaranteed error on the quality of the abstractions. Among other goals, we are investigating issues of decentralised control of such PV, of emergence of global behaviours from local conditions, and in general issues of robustness, dependability, and reliability over the grid.

6   Conclusions

The increase in complexity, adaptability, and inter-connectivity of modern technological devices raises new challenges towards their understanding and that of their complex interaction network. Likewise, their local actuation or the control of the global network they are part of, pose new challenges at engineering and technical levels. We have argued for the necessary development of formal verification approaches to study networks of complex dynamical systems, underpinned by quantitative models that are at the core stochastic and hybrid, built from data and formally reasoned upon.

We envision the development of semi-automatic approaches, based on formal abstractions, for the synthesis of policies around quantitative specifications encompassing formal requirements (e.g., safety, reliability), and trading off against performance, as well as the development of formal verification tools accounting for robustness. Such approaches are deemed "formal" in that they are enhanced by quantitative guarantees on their outcomes, being it an assertion over a formal property or the implementation of a control policy towards a given objective.

Furthermore, in view of the unavoidable connection of the systems of interest with data, we have further advocated more research on a tighter and formal integration of data-driven, sample-based approaches, with model-based deductive techniques: we view this integration as necessary not only to encompass adaptability features for the underlying models towards learning, but also to increase the scalability of formal verification techniques towards reasoning.

In conclusion, the technical challenges related to the existing technological trend towards more complex, adaptable and more integrated devices, can be offset by engineering and economic benefits, provided principled approaches for integrated data-based modelling, quantitative formal verification, and correct-by-design synthesis are embraced.

Acknowledgments. This is a position article accompanying a keynote talk at NSV 2016. It exclusively portrays the perspective of the author, without claims of generality or comprehensiveness. As such, references are limited to own work.

The author would like to thank former and current students involved in this specific area of work, particularly Sofie Haesaert, Sadegh E.S. Soudjani, and Majid Zamani; and collaborators on these topics, particularly Martie Fränzle, Joost-Pieter Katoen, Daniel Kroening, Marta Kwiatkovska, John Lygeros, Rupak Majumdar, Maria Prandini, and Claire Tomlin.

References

1. Abate, A.: Approximation metrics based on probabilistic bisimulations for general state-space Markov processes: a survey. Electron. Notes Theor. Comput. Sci. **297**, 3–25 (2012)
2. Abate, A., D'Innocenzo, A., Di Benedetto, M.D.: Approximate abstractions of stochastic hybrid systems. IEEE Trans. Autom. Control **56**(11), 2688–2694 (2011)
3. Abate, A., Katoen, J.-P., Lygeros, J., Prandini, M.: Approximate model checking of stochastic hybrid systems. Eur. J. Control **6**, 624–641 (2010)
4. Abate, A., Kwiatkowska, M., Norman, G., Parker, D.: Probabilistic model checking of labelled markov processes via finite approximate bisimulations. In: Breugel, F., Kashefi, E., Palamidessi, C., Rutten, J. (eds.) Horizons of the Mind. A Tribute to Prakash Panangaden. LNCS, vol. 8464, pp. 40–58. Springer, Heidelberg (2014). doi:10.1007/978-3-319-06880-0_2
5. Abate, A., Prandini, M., Lygeros, J., Sastry, S.: Probabilistic reachability and safety for controlled discrete time stochastic hybrid systems. Automatica **44**(11), 2724–2734 (2008)
6. Various authors. FP7 AMBI project. http://www.ambi-project.eu
7. Various authors. FP7 MoVeS project. http://www.movesproject.eu
8. Ding, J., Kamgarpour, M., Summers, S., Abate, A., Lygeros, J., Tomlin, C.J.: A stochastic games framework for verification and control of discrete-time stochastic hybrid systems. Automatica **49**(9), 2665–2674 (2013)
9. Esmaeil Zadeh Soudjani, S., Abate, A.: Adaptive and sequential gridding procedures for the abstraction and verification of stochastic processes. SIAM J. Appl. Dyn. Syst. **12**(2), 921–956 (2013)
10. Esmaeil Zadeh Soudjani, S., Abate, A.: Aggregation of thermostatically controlled loads by formal abstractions. In: European Control Conference, Zurich, Switzerland, pp. 4232–4237, July 2013
11. Esmaeil Zadeh Soudjani, S., Abate, A.: Precise approximations of the probability distribution of a Markov process in time: an application to probabilistic invariance. In: Ábrahám, E., Havelund, K. (eds.) TACAS 2014. LNCS, vol. 8413, pp. 547–561. Springer, Heidelberg (2014). doi:10.1007/978-3-642-54862-8_45
12. Esmaeil Zadeh Soudjani, S., Abate, A.: Probabilistic reach-avoid computation for partially-degenerate stochastic processes. IEEE Trans. Autom. Control **59**(2), 528–534 (2014)
13. Soudjani, S.E.Z., Gevaerts, C., Abate, A.: FAUST^2: formal abstractions of uncountable-state stochastic processes. In: Baier, C., Tinelli, C. (eds.) TACAS 2015. LNCS, vol. 9035, pp. 272–286. Springer, Heidelberg (2015). doi:10.1007/978-3-662-46681-0_23
14. Haesaert, S., Abate, A., Van Den Hof, P.M.J.: Data-driven and model-based verification: a Bayesian identification approach. In: Proceedings of the IEEE Conference on Decision and Control, pp. 6830–6835 (2016)
15. Haesaert, S., Abate, A., Hof, P.M.J.: Verification of general Markov decision processes by approximate similarity relations and policy refinement. In: Agha, G., Houdt, B. (eds.) QEST 2016. LNCS, vol. 9826, pp. 227–243. Springer, Heidelberg (2016). doi:10.1007/978-3-319-43425-4_16
16. Kamgarpour, M., Ellen, C., Esmaeil Zadeh Soudjani, S., Gerwinn, S., Mathieu, J.L., Mullner, N., Abate, A., Callaway, D.S., Fränzle, M., Lygeros, J.: Modeling options for demand side participation of thermostatically controlled loads. In: International Conference on Bulk Power System Dynamics and Control (IREP), pp. 1–15, August 2013

17. Esmaeil Zadeh Soudjani, S., Abate, A.: Quantitative approximation of the probability distribution of a Markov process by formal abstractions. Logical Methods Comput. Sci. **11**(3), 1–29 (2015)
18. Tkachev, I., Abate, A.: Characterization and computation of infinite-horizon specifications over Markov processes. Theoret. Comput. Sci. **515**, 1–18 (2014)
19. Tkachev, I., Mereacre, A., Katoen, J.-P., Abate, A.: Quantitative model checking of controlled discrete-time Markov processes. Inform. Comput. (2016). doi:10.1016/j.ic.2016.11.006
20. Zamani, M., Abate, A.: Symbolic models for randomly switched stochastic systems. Syst. Control Lett. **69**, 38–46 (2014)
21. Zamani, M., Abate, A., Girard, A.: Symbolic models for stochastic switched systems: a discretization and a discretization-free approach. Automatica **55**(5), 183–196 (2015)
22. Zamani, M., Mohajerin Esfahani, P., Majumdar, R., Abate, A., Lygeros, J.: Symbolic control of stochastic systems via approximately bisimilar finite abstractions. IEEE Trans. Autom. Control **59**(12), 2825–2830 (2014)
23. Zamani, M., Mazo, M., Abate, A.: Finite abstractions of networked control systems. In: Proceedings of the 53rd IEEE Conference on Decision and Control, pp. 95–100 (2014)

Proving Properties on PWA Systems Using Copositive and Semidefinite Programming

Assalé Adjé[✉]

Institut de Recherche en Informatique de Toulouse, Université Paul Sabatier,
Toulouse, France
assale.adje@irit.fr

Abstract. In this paper, we present a model based on copositive programming and semidefinite relaxations of it to prove properties on discrete-time piecewise affine systems. We consider invariant i.e. properties represented by a set and formulated as all reachable values are included in the set. Also, we restrict the analysis to sublevel sets of quadratic forms i.e. ellipsoids. In this case, to check the property is equivalent to solve a quadratic maximization problem under the constraint that the decision variable belongs to the reachable values set. This maximization problem is relaxed using an abstraction of reachable values set by a union of truncated ellipsoids.

1 Introduction

The formal verification aims to prove automatically some properties on dynamical systems. In our paper, we are interested in proving invariant i.e. a property valid for all reachable values without regarding the step when we reach the value. In our point-of-view, a property can be represented by a set C. Checking the property can be reduced to check whether the set of the reachable values is fully contained in C. The paper proposes a static analysis framework to solve the verification problem. In other words, we develop a technique to check the property without any system simulation. In this paper, we handle properties representable as a sublevel of a quadratic function i.e. an ellipsoid. The verification problem in this case is equivalent to solving an optimization problem where the decision variable is constrained to belong to the reachable values set. One may think that to solve the problem, it suffices to represent precisely the reachable values set to check the property. Nevertheless, classically, in static analysis, the reachable values set is approached iteratively using Kleene iterations scheme. Since the computation is slow, Kleene iterations are coupled with acceleration techniques that degrades the representation of the reachable values set. Thus the verification of property may fail because of the loss of precision. In this paper, we use a direct method based on semidefinite programming to represent the reachable

The author has been supported by the CIMI (Centre International de Mathématiques et d'Informatique) Excellence program ANR-11-LABX-0040-CIMI within the program ANR-11-IDEX-0002-02 during a postdoctoral fellowship.

S. Bogomolov et al. (Eds.): NSV 2016, LNCS 10152, pp. 15–30, 2017.
DOI: 10.1007/978-3-319-54292-8_2

values set and check the property in the same time. The main idea is to use a minimizing abstraction based on union of truncated ellipsoids.

Related Works. This method is an adaptation of [2]. Indeed in [2], we propose the synthesis of a minimizing polynomial sublevel abstraction based on sums-of-squares. Here, we allow non-polynomial abstraction but we restrict ourselves to semidefinite programming to have a better scalability. The method proposed here is also an extension of [1] since in [1], the only property handled is the boundedness.

The techniques presented in this paper uses piecewise quadratic Lyapunov conditions [9,12]. However, in [9,12], the authors are interested in proving stability of piecewise affine systems. As classical quadratic Lyapunov functions, piecewise quadratic Lyapunov functions provide sublevel invariant sets to the system. We use this latter interpretation for a verification purpose. In this paper, we are interesting in synthezing disjunctive invariants. This form of invariants appears for tropical polyhedra domain [3] where the author generates disjunctions of zones as invariants. The latter invariants did not encode quadratic relations between variables. The synthesis of quadratic invariants for switched systems is studied in [4]. But, the invariants generation is not guided by property or is not relied on optimization problems.

Organisation of the Paper. The paper is organised as follows. In Sect. 2, we present the context that is the systems and the properties that we consider in the paper. Then in Sect. 3, we give detail about the mathematical model using semidefinite programming to solve optimization problems. In Sect. 4, we conclude and propose some future works.

2 Proving Properties on Constrained Piecewise Affine Discrete-Time Dynamical Systems

2.1 Some Recalls About Polyhedra

In this paper, we will denote by $\mathbb{M}_{n \times m}$ the set of matrices with n rows and m columns. For $n \in \mathbb{N}$, $[n]$ will denote the set of integers $\{1, \dots, n\}$.

In our work, we suppose that a (convex) polyhedron can contain both strict and weak inequalities.

Definition 1 (Polyhedra of $\mathbb{R}^d$). *A polyhedron of $\mathbb{R}^d$ is a set of the form:*

$$\{x \in \mathbb{R}^d \,|\, P_s x \ll b_s, \ P_w x \le b_w\}$$

where $P_s \in \mathbb{M}_{n_s \times d}$, $P_w \in \mathbb{M}_{n_w \times d}$, $b_s \in \mathbb{R}^{n_s}$ and $b_w \in \mathbb{R}^{n_w}$. We insist on the notation: $y \ll z$ means that for all coordinates l, $y_l < z_l$ and $y \le z$ means that for all coordinates l, $y_l \le z_l$.

Lemma 1 (Polyhedra closure). *The topological closure of a nonempty or a nontrivial (not $\mathbb{R}^d$) polyhedron consists in keeping weak inequalities and replacing strict inequalities by weak inequalities.*

The direct application of Motzkin's transposition theorem [13] yields to the next proposition.

Proposition 1 (Test of the emptyness of a polyhedra). *Let X be a polyhedra. Suppose that $X = \{x \in \mathbb{R}^d \,|\, P_s x \ll b_s, \; P_w x \leq b_w\}$. Then $X \neq \emptyset$ if and only if:*

$$
\begin{cases}
\begin{pmatrix} 1 & 0_{1 \times d} \\ b_s & -P_s \end{pmatrix}^{\mathsf{T}} p^s + \begin{pmatrix} b_w & -P_w \end{pmatrix}^{\mathsf{T}} p = 0 \\[2ex]
\sum_{k=1}^{n_s+1} p_k^s = 1, \; p^s \geq 0, \; p \geq 0
\end{cases}
$$

has no solution.

Definition 2 (Indices of meeting polyhedra). *We consider L finite families of polyhedra $(S^i)_{i \in [L]}$. For all $i \in [L]$, $S^i = \{X_1^i, \ldots, X_{N_i}^i\}$. We define:*

$$
\mathrm{Com}(S^1, S^2, \ldots, S^L) = \{(i_1, i_2, \ldots, i_L) \in \prod_{i=1}^{L} [N_i] \mid \bigcap_{j=1}^{L} X_{i_j}^j \neq \emptyset\}.
$$

Corollary 1. *Let $(S^i)_{i \in [L]}$ be L finite families of polyhedra. Suppose that for all $i \in [L]$, S^i has N^i elements. Then $\mathrm{Com}(S^1, S^2, \ldots, S^L)$ can be computed using $\prod_{i=1}^{L} N^i$ linear systems.*

Definition 3 (Polyhedric partition). *A polyhedric partition is a family of polyhedra of $\mathbb{R}^d$, $\{X^1, \ldots, X^N\}$ such that:*

$$
\forall i, j \in [N], \text{s.t.}\, i \neq j, \; X^i \cap X^j = \emptyset \quad and \quad \bigcup_{i \in [N]} X^i = \mathbb{R}^d .
$$

If a polyhedric partition S contains N elements, we will say that S is a polyhedric partition of size N.

We will denote by $f_{|X}$ the restriction of a function $f : X \mapsto \mathbb{R}^m$ on the set X.

Definition 4 (Piecewise affine maps). *A map $f : \mathbb{R}^d \to \mathbb{R}^m$ is piecewise affine if and only if there exists a polyhedric partition $\{X^i, i \in [N]\}$ such that $f_{|X^i}$ is affine.*

Definition 5 (Piecewise quadratic functions). *A function $f : \mathbb{R}^d \to \mathbb{R}$ is piecewise quadratic if and only if there exists a polyhedric partition $\{X^i, i \in [N]\}$ such that $f_{|X^i}$ is quadratic.*

2.2 Piecewise Affine Discrete-Time Systems

In this paper, we are interested in proving automatically properties on piecewise affine discrete-time systems (PWA for short). The term piecewise affine means that the dynamic of the system is piecewise affine. From Definition 4, there exists a polyhedric partition $\{X^i, i \in \mathcal{I}\}$ such that for all $i \in \mathcal{I}$, the dynamic of the system restricted to X^i is affine. The dynamic of a PWA is thus represented by the following relation for all $k \in \mathbb{N}$, for all $i \in \mathcal{I}$:

$$\text{if } x_k \in X^i, \ x_{k+1} = f^i(x_k), \ f^i : y \mapsto A^i y + b^i \tag{1}$$

where $A^i \in \mathbb{M}_{d \times d}$ and b^i a vector of $\mathbb{R}^d$. We assume that the initial condition x_0 belongs to some polytope X^{in}. We will need homogeneous versions of laws and thus introduce the $(1 + d) \times (1 + d)$ matrices F^i defined as follows:

$$F^i = \begin{pmatrix} 1 & 0_{1 \times d} \\ b^i & A^i \end{pmatrix}. \tag{2}$$

The system defined in Eq. (1) can be rewritten as $(1, x_{k+1})^\intercal = F^i(1, x_k)$.

To sum up, we give a formal definition of what we call a piecewise affine system (PWA for short).

Definition 6 (Piecewise Affine System). *A piecewise affine system (PWA) is the triple $(X^{\text{in}}, \mathcal{X}, \mathcal{A})$ where:*

- *X^{in} is the polytope of the possible initial conditions;*
- *$\mathcal{X} := \{X^i, i \in \mathcal{I}\}$ is the polyhedral partition;*
- *$\mathcal{A} := \{f^i, i \in \mathcal{I}\}$ is the family of affine laws relative to $\mathcal{X}$ satisfying Eq. (1).*

Example 1 (Running example). Let us consider the piecewise linear system depicted in [12]. We bring some modifications: we complete the example by adding a nondeterministic initial condition and we slighty change the partition used in [12], to satisfy Definition 3.

Let us take $X^{\text{in}} = [-1, 1] \times [-1, 1]$. The dynamical system is defined, for all $k \in \mathbb{N}$, by

$$x_{k+1} = \begin{cases} A^1 x_k & \text{if } \begin{cases} x_{k,1} \geq 0 \\ x_{k,2} \geq 0 \end{cases} \\ A^2 x_k & \text{if } \begin{cases} x_{k,1} \geq 0 \\ x_{k,2} < 0 \end{cases} \\ A^3 x_k & \text{if } \begin{cases} x_{k,1} < 0 \\ x_{k,2} < 0 \end{cases} \\ A^4 x_k & \text{if } \begin{cases} x_{k,1} < 0 \\ x_{k,2} \geq 0 \end{cases} \end{cases}$$

with

$$A^1 = \begin{pmatrix} -0.04 & -0.461 \\ -0.139 & 0.341 \end{pmatrix}, \ A^2 = \begin{pmatrix} 0.936 & 0.323 \\ 0.788 & -0.049 \end{pmatrix}$$

$$A^3 = \begin{pmatrix} -0.857 & 0.815 \\ 0.491 & 0.62 \end{pmatrix}, \ A^4 = \begin{pmatrix} -0.022 & 0.644 \\ 0.758 & 0.271 \end{pmatrix}$$

We thus have

$$X^1 = \{x \in \mathbb{R}^2 \mid -x_1 \leq 0, -x_2 \leq 0\}, \ X^2 = \{x \in \mathbb{R}^2 \mid -x_1 \leq 0, x_2 < 0\},$$
$$X^3 = \{x \in \mathbb{R}^2 \mid x_1 < 0, x_2 < 0\} \text{ and } X^4 = \{x \in \mathbb{R}^2 \mid x_1 < 0, -x_2 \leq 0\}.$$

Now, we formally define the set of reachable values.

Definition 7 (Reachable values set). *Let $P = (X^{\text{in}}, \mathcal{X}, \mathcal{A})$ be a PWA. We define the reachable values set as the set $\mathcal{R}_P$ defined by:*

$$\mathcal{R}_P = \bigcup_{k \in \mathbb{N}} \mathbb{A}^k(X^{\text{in}}), \text{ where } \mathbb{A} : \mathbb{R}^d \mapsto \mathbb{R}^d, \mathbb{A}(x) = A^i x + b^i \text{ if } x \in X^i$$

In Definition 7, we put P in index, but in the rest of the paper we simply write $\mathcal{R}$ since there will be no confusion.

Example 2 (Reachable values of the running example). Figure 1 depicts a discretized version of the reachable values set of Example 1. Actually, the set of intial conditions X^{in} is discretized. The discretization step is of 0.2. Then the trajectory starting from a point in the discretization of X^{in} is drawn. The trajectories are stopped at exactly 100 runs.

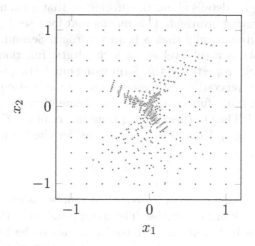

Fig. 1. A discrete version of the reachable values set of Example 1

Definition 8 (Invariant). *Let $P = (X^{\text{in}}, \mathcal{X}, \mathcal{A})$ be a PWA. A set $S \subseteq \mathbb{R}^d$ is a said to be an invariant if and only if $\mathcal{R}_P \subseteq S$.*

Example 3 (An invariant for the running example). Figure 2 depicts an invariant computed as the sublevel of a piecewise quadratic function. We will come back later on the details of its computation at Subsect. 3.5.

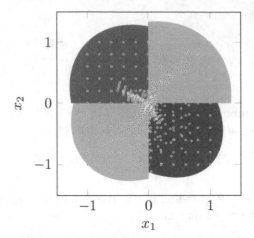

Fig. 2. An invariant sublevel of a piecewise quadratic function for Example 1, in yellow, the set of Example 2 (Color figure online)

2.3 Proving Properties on PWA

In this section, we give details about the properties that we can handle. First, we are interested in proving invariant. This means that for a set S given by the user, we aim to prove automatically that S is an invariant. Second, we only consider sets S representable as a sublevel set of a quadratic function i.e. an ellipsoid. Indeed, we can check properties of this form using quadratic programming. Then we use semi-definite relaxations of the constructed quadratic programs.

Let V be a quadratic function and let us define $S = \{x \in \mathbb{R}^d \mid V(x) \leq \alpha\}$ which is an ellipsoid. Then to check that S is an invariant i.e. $\mathcal{R} \subseteq S$ is equivalent to solve to check $\sup_{x \in \mathcal{R}} V(x) \leq \alpha$. Let us consider the following optimization problem:

$$\sup_{x \in \mathcal{R}} x^\mathsf{T} M x + 2p^\mathsf{T} x \tag{3}$$

To determine the optimal value of Problem (3) represents exactly the work that we have to do to check our properties. The main problem in Problem (3) is that we cannot use $\mathcal{R}$ as in Definition 7. Actually $\mathcal{R}$ cannot be implementable and we propose to use an implementable over-approximation of $\mathcal{R}$. This principle is not new and corresponds to the concept of abstract interpretation. We refer the reader to [7] for a seminal presentation of this approach. We can characterize $\mathcal{R}$ as the collecting semantics i.e. the smallest fixed point of a transfer function. Let us denote by $\wp(\mathbb{R}^d)$ the set of subsets of $\mathbb{R}^d$. The transfer function $F : \wp(\mathbb{R}^d) \to \wp(\mathbb{R}^d)$ we use is defined as follows:

$$F(C) = X^{\text{in}} \cup \bigcup_{i \in \mathcal{I}} f^i \left(C \cap X^i \right) \tag{4}$$

We equip $\wp(\mathbb{R}^d)$ with the partial order of inclusion. The infimum is understood in this sense i.e. as the greatest lower bound with respect to this order. The smallest fixed point problem is:

$$\inf \left\{ C \in \wp(\mathbb{R}^d) \mid C = F(C) \right\}.$$

It is well-known from Tarski's theorem that the solution of this problem exists, is unique and in this case, it corresponds to $\mathcal{R}$. Tarski's theorem also states that $\mathcal{R}$ is the smallest solution of the following Problem:

$$\inf \left\{ C \in \wp(\mathbb{R}^d) \mid F(C) \subseteq C \right\}.$$

Finally, any set P^{ind} such that $F(P^{\mathrm{ind}}) \subseteq P^{\mathrm{ind}}$ provides a safe over-approximation of $\mathcal{R}$. In this case, such P^{ind} is called *inductive invariant*. An abstraction consists in restricting the family of inductive invariants P^{ind} to an implementable one. Here, we chose to constraint an inductive invariant to be a sublevel of a piecewise quadratic function. Indeed, to be inductive is equivalent to asking a Lyapunov condition for sets. Moreover, the sublevels of a Lyapunov function are inductive invariants if and only if they contain initial conditions. In the context of piecewise affine systems, the class of piecewise quadratic functions furnishes a relevant class of Lyapunov functions [9,12]. Consequently, to solve Problem (3), we will compute a piecewise quadratic function V^{ind} such that the sublevel set $S^{\mathrm{ind}} = \{x \in \mathbb{R}^d \mid V^{\mathrm{ind}}(x) \leq 0\}$:

$$\text{is an inductive invariant i.e. } F(S^{\mathrm{ind}}) \subseteq S^{\mathrm{ind}} \tag{5}$$

$$\text{minimizes the value } \sup_{x \in S^{\mathrm{ind}}} x^{\mathsf{T}} M x + 2 p^{\mathsf{T}} x \tag{6}$$

Example 4 (The boundedness problem). To prove automatically that the reachable values set $\mathcal{R}$ of the running example is bounded, we have to solve the optimization problem:

$$\sup_{(x_1, x_2) \in \mathcal{R}} x_1^2 + x_2^2$$

If the problem has a finite optimal value then $\mathcal{R}$ is bounded. Following, Eqs. (5) and (6), we should look for a piecewise quadratic function such that the 0-sublevel set S^{ind} provides an overapproximation of $\mathcal{R}$ which minimizes the error between the $\sup_{(x_1, x_2) \in \mathcal{R}} x_1^2 + x_2^2$ and $\sup_{(x_1, x_2) \in S^{\mathrm{ind}}} x_1^2 + x_2^2$.

3   The Mathematical Model

Now we give the details about the computation of the piecewise quadratic function V^{ind} such that S^{ind} satisfies Eqs. (5) and (6). First we introduce the notion of cone-copositive matrices.

3.1   Cone-Copositive Matrices

The set $\mathbb{S}_m$ denotes the set of symmetric matrices. The set $\mathbb{S}_m^+$ denotes the set of (symmetric) positive semidefinite matrices i.e. the matrices A such that $x^\mathsf{T} A x \geq 0$ for all $x \in \mathbb{R}^m$. When the dimension of the matrices is obvious we will also use the notation $A \succeq 0$ for A is positive semidefinite. The set $\mathbb{S}_m^{\geq 0}$ denotes the set of symmetric matrices with nonnegative coefficients.

Let q be a quadratic form i.e. a function such that for all $y \in \mathbb{R}^d$, $q(y) = y^\mathsf{T} A_q y + b_q^\mathsf{T} y + c_q$ where $A_q \in \mathbb{S}_d$, $b_q \in \mathbb{R}^d$ and $c_q \in \mathbb{R}$. We define the lift-matrix of q, the matrix of $\mathbb{S}_{d+1}$ defined as follows:

$$\mathbf{M}(A_q, b_q, c_q) = \mathbf{M}(q) = \begin{pmatrix} c_q & (b_q/2)^\mathsf{T} \\ (b_q/2) & A_q \end{pmatrix} \tag{7}$$

It is obvious that the $q \mapsto \mathbf{M}(q)$ is linear. Let $A \in \mathbb{M}_{d \times d}$, $b \in \mathbb{R}^d$, and q be a quadratic form, we have, for all $x \in \mathbb{R}^d$:

$$q(Ax + b) = \begin{pmatrix} 1 \\ x \end{pmatrix}^\mathsf{T} \begin{pmatrix} 1 & 0_{1 \times d} \\ b & A \end{pmatrix}^\mathsf{T} \mathbf{M}(q) \begin{pmatrix} 1 & 0_{1 \times d} \\ b & A \end{pmatrix} \begin{pmatrix} 1 \\ x \end{pmatrix}. \tag{8}$$

Lemma 2. *Let $A \in \mathbb{S}_d$, $b \in \mathbb{R}^d$ and $c \in \mathbb{R}$. Then: $(\forall y \in \mathbb{R}^d, \ y^\mathsf{T} A y + b^\mathsf{T} y + c \geq 0) \iff \mathbf{M}(A, b, c) \in \mathbb{S}_{d+1}^+$*

Definition 9 ((Cone)-copositive matrices). *Let $M \in \mathbb{M}_{m \times d}$. A matrix $Q \in \mathbb{S}_d$ which satisfies*

$$My \geq 0 \implies y^\mathsf{T} Q y \geq 0$$

is called M-copositive.

An Id_d-copositive matrix is called a copositive matrix. We denote by $\mathbf{C}_d(M)$ the set of M-copositive matrices and $\mathbf{C}_d$ the set of copositive matrices.

Lemma 3. *A quadratic function q is nonnegative over a polyhedron P if and only if q is nonnegative on the topological closure of P.*

For $P \in \mathbb{M}_{n \times m}$ and $c \in \mathbb{R}^n$, we define the following matrix:

$$\mathbf{H}(P, c) = \begin{pmatrix} 1 & 0_{1 \times m} \\ c & -P \end{pmatrix} \in \mathbb{M}_{(n+1) \times (m+1)} \tag{9}$$

We also use the notation $\mathbf{H}(C)$ for a polyhedron C with the same meaning i.e. if $C = \{x \in \mathbb{R}^d \mid P_s x \ll b_s, \ P_w x \leq b_w\}$ and we have $P = \begin{pmatrix} P_s \\ P_w \end{pmatrix}$ and $b = \begin{pmatrix} b_s \\ b_w \end{pmatrix}$, then $\mathbf{H}(C) = \mathbf{H}(P, b)$.

Lemma 4. *Let $P \in \mathbb{M}_{n \times m}$ and $c \in \mathbb{R}^n$. Then, for all $x \in \mathbb{R}^n$, $Px \leq c \iff \mathbf{H}(P, c) \begin{pmatrix} 1 \\ x \end{pmatrix} \geq 0$.*

Lemma 5. *Let $q : \mathbb{R}^d \to \mathbb{R}^d$ be a quadratic function and C be a polyhedron. Then $\mathbf{M}(q) \in \mathbf{C}_{d+1}(\mathbf{H}(C)) \implies (q(x) \geq 0, \forall x \in C)$.*

Cone-copositive matrix characterizations is an intensive research field and a list of interesting papers about can be found in [5].

Proposition 2 (Theorem 2.1 of [10]). *Let $M \in \mathbb{M}_{m \times d}$. Then:*

$$\{ M^\mathsf{T} C M + S \mid C \in \mathbf{C}_d \text{ and } S \in \mathbb{S}_d^+ \} \subseteq \mathbf{C}_d(M) \qquad (\Delta)$$

If the rank of M is equal to m, then (Δ) is actually an equality.

The next proposition discusses simple a characterization of copositive matrices as a sum of a semi-definite positive matrix and a nonnegative matrix.

Proposition 3 ([8,11]). *We have: $\forall d \in \mathbb{N}$: $\mathbb{S}_d^{\geq 0} + \mathbb{S}_d^+ \subseteq \mathbf{C}_d$. If $d \leq 4$ then $\mathbf{C}_d = \mathbb{S}_d^{\geq 0} + \mathbb{S}_d^+$.*

Corollary 2. *Let $M \in \mathbb{M}_{m \times d}$. Then:*

$$\mathbf{C}_d(M) \supseteq \left\{ Q \in \mathbb{S}_d \;\middle|\; \begin{array}{l} \exists\, W_p \in \mathbb{S}_m^{\geq 0},\; W_+ \in \mathbb{S}_m^+,\; \text{s.t.} \\ Q - M^\mathsf{T}(W_p + W_+) M \succeq 0 \end{array} \right\} \qquad (\star)$$

If M has full row rank and $d \leq 4$, then $(\star)$ is actually an equality.

Copositive constraints study is a quite recent field of research. Algorithms exist (e.g. [6]) but for the knowledge of the author no tools are available. In this paper, in practice, we use Corollary 2 and we replace $\mathbf{C}_d(M)$ by the right-hand side of Eq. $(\star)$.

Example 5 (Why is there $(1, 0_{1 \times d})$ in $\mathbf{H}(P, c)?$). Consider $X = \{ x \in \mathbb{R} \mid x \leq 1 \}$. Let $u(x) = (1, x)$, and $M = (1\ -1)$ (this corresponds to $\mathbf{H}(1, 1)$ without $(1, 0)$). Then $X = \{ x \mid Mu(x)^\mathsf{T} \geq 0 \}$.

In $\mathbb{R}$, positive semidefinite matrices and matrices with nonnegative coefficients define the same set that is the set of nonnegative reals. Now let $W \geq 0$ and define $X' = \{ x \mid u(x) M^\mathsf{T} W M u(x)^\mathsf{T} \geq 0 \}$. Since $u(x) M^\mathsf{T} W M u(x)^\mathsf{T} = W u(x) M^\mathsf{T} M u(x)^\mathsf{T} = 2W(1 - x)^2$, $X' = \mathbb{R}$ for all $W \geq 0$.

Now let us take $E = \mathbf{H}(1, 1)$ and let $W = \left(\begin{smallmatrix} w_1 & w_3 \\ w_3 & w_2 \end{smallmatrix} \right)$ with $w_1, w_2, w_3 \geq 0$ and define $\overline{X} = \{ x \mid u(x) E^\mathsf{T} W E u(x)^\mathsf{T} \geq 0 \}$. Hence, $u(x) E^\mathsf{T} \left(\begin{smallmatrix} w_1 & w_3 \\ w_3 & w_2 \end{smallmatrix} \right) E u(x)^\mathsf{T} = w_1 + 2w_3(1 - x) + w_2(1 - x)^2$. Taking for example $w_2 = w_1 = 0$ and $w_3 > 0$ implies that $\overline{X} = X$. Note that, in this case, we can choose the positive semidefinite certificate equal to $\left(\begin{smallmatrix} 0 & 0 \\ 0 & 0 \end{smallmatrix} \right)$.

3.2 Inductiveness

Come back to the invariant proof. Recall that we are looking for a sublevel of a piecewise quadratic function that overapproximate $\mathcal{R}_P$ that minimizes the abstraction. Since, we are interested in a piecewise quadratic function, we need a polyhedric partition. Let us denote by $\mathcal{S} = (S^1, \ldots, S^n)$ the unknown polyhedric partition. We associate for all indices $i \in [n]$ of the partition, a quadratic form $x \mapsto x^\mathsf{T} P^i x + 2x^\mathsf{T} q^i + r^i$. Then, we have:

$$S^{\mathrm{ind}} = \bigcup_{i \in [n]} S^{i,\mathrm{ind}} \text{ where } S^{i,\mathrm{ind}} = \{x \in S^i \mid x^\mathsf{T} P^i x + 2x^\mathsf{T} q^i + r^i \leq 0\} \quad (10)$$

Lemma 6 (Partial S-Lemma). *Let q_1, q_2 be two quadratic forms over $\mathbb{R}^m$ and C be a polyhedron of $\mathbb{R}^m$. If the following assertion*

$$(\exists \lambda \in \mathbb{R}_+,\ y \in C \implies \lambda q_1(y) - q_2(y) \geq 0)$$

holds then the following assertion

$$(y \in C \wedge q_1(y) \leq 0 \implies q_2(y) \leq 0)$$

is true.

Remark 1. If Lemma 6, q_1 and $-q_2$ are convex and there exists $x_0 \in \mathbb{R}^m$ which belongs to the interior of C and satisfies $q_1(x_0) < 0$ then the two assertions of Lemma 6 are equivalent.

We now write SDP conditions to constraint S^{ind} to satisfy $F(S^{\mathrm{ind}}) \subseteq S^{\mathrm{ind}}$. Recall that $F(C) = X^{\mathrm{in}} \cup \bigcup_{i \in \mathcal{I}} f^i (C \cap X^i)$. So $F(S^{\mathrm{ind}}) \subseteq S^{\mathrm{ind}}$ if and only if:

$$X^{\mathrm{in}} \subseteq S^{\mathrm{ind}} \text{ and } \forall i \in \mathcal{I},\ f^i (X^i \cap S^{\mathrm{ind}}) \subseteq S^{\mathrm{ind}}$$

First, let us consider $X^{\mathrm{in}} \subseteq S^{\mathrm{ind}}$. We use the polyhedric partition $\mathcal{S}$ to decompose X^{in} in subproblems $X^{\mathrm{in}} \cap S^i \subseteq S^{\mathrm{ind}}$. Then, we use the fact that for $i \neq j$, $S^i \cap S^j = \emptyset$ and then $X^{\mathrm{in}} \cap S^i$ cannot meet S^j for $j \neq i$. Hence, we have $X^{\mathrm{in}} \cap S^i \subseteq S^{\mathrm{ind}}$ if and only if $X^{\mathrm{in}} \cap S^i \subseteq S^{i,\mathrm{ind}}$. Finally, from Eq. (10), $X^{\mathrm{in}} \subseteq S^{\mathrm{ind}}$ is equivalent to, for all $i \in \mathrm{Com}(\{X^{\mathrm{in}}\}, \mathcal{S})$,

$$-x^\mathsf{T} P^i x - 2x^\mathsf{T} q^i - r^i \geq 0, \forall x \in X^{\mathrm{in}} \cap S^i$$

Recall that X^{in} and S^i are both polyhedra, the constraint on S^{ind}, $X^{\mathrm{in}} \subseteq S^{\mathrm{ind}}$ is equivalent on a finite number of constraints imposing the positivity of a quadratic form over a known polyhedron. Then, we can reinforce the constraint by applying Lemma 5 and finally to constraint S^{ind} to satisfy $X^{\mathrm{in}} \subseteq S^{\mathrm{ind}}$, we impose:

$$\forall i \in \mathrm{Com}(\{X^{\mathrm{in}}\}, \mathcal{S}),\ \mathbf{M}(-P^i, -2q^i, -r^i) \in \mathbf{C}_{d+1} (\mathbf{H} (X^{\mathrm{in}} \cap S^i)). \quad (11)$$

Now, we study the second constraint that is for all $i \in \mathcal{I}$, $f^i (X^i \cap S^{\mathrm{ind}}) \subseteq S^{\mathrm{ind}}$. For $i \in \mathcal{I}$, we write:

$$(f^i)^{-1}(\mathcal{S}) = \{(f^i)^{-1}(S^1), \ldots, (f^i)^{-1}(S^n)\},$$

this forms a polyhedric partition of $\mathbb{R}^d$ since $\mathcal{S}$ is. Let $i \in \mathcal{I}$. We use the same principle as for $X^{\mathrm{in}} \subseteq S^{\mathrm{ind}}$ and we decompose $f^i (X^i \cap S^{\mathrm{ind}})$ using the polyhedric partition $\mathcal{S}$. First from Eq. (10) and since the direct image of union is the union of image, we have $f^i \left(X^i \cap S^{\text{ind}} \right) = \cup_{j \in [n]} f^i \left(X^i \cap S^{j,\text{ind}} \right)$. Then we use the fact that S is a polyhedric partition, we get $f^i \left(X^i \cap S^{\text{ind}} \right) = \cup_{k \in [n]} \cup_{j \in [n]} f^i \left(X^i \cap S^{j,\text{ind}} \right) \cap S^k$. Again, from the fact that the polyhedra S^ks cannot meet each others, we conclude that $f^i \left(X^i \cap S^{j,\text{ind}} \right) \cap S^k \subseteq S^{\text{ind}}$ if and only if $f^i \left(X^i \cap S^{j,\text{ind}} \right) \cap S^k \subseteq S^{k,\text{ind}}$. Finally, we can restrict the indices (j,k) to those such that (i,j,k) belongs $\text{Com}(\mathcal{X}, \mathcal{S}, f^{i^{-1}}(\mathcal{S}))$. In conclusion, the statement: for all $i \in \mathcal{I}$, $f^i \left(X^i \cap S^{\text{ind}} \right) \subseteq S^{\text{ind}}$, is equivalent to:

$$\forall \, i \in \mathcal{I}, \; \forall \, (j,k) \in [n]^2 \text{ s.t. } (i,j,k) \in \text{Com}(\mathcal{X}, \mathcal{S}, f^{i^{-1}}(\mathcal{S})),$$
$$\forall \, x \in X^i \cap S^{j,\text{ind}} \cap (f^i)^{-1}(S^k), \; f^i(x)^\mathsf{T} P^k f^i(x) + 2 f^i(x)^\mathsf{T} q^k + r^k \leq 0. \quad (12)$$

Note that $S^{j,\text{ind}}$ is actually the intersection of the polyhedron S^j and the ellipsoid $\{x \mid x^\mathsf{T} P^j x + 2 x^\mathsf{T} q^j + r^j \leq 0\}$ and thus the constraint $x \in S^{j,\text{ind}}$ is the conjonction of affine constraints and a quadratic constraint. Moreover, $X^i \cap S^j \cap (f^i)^{-1}(S^k)$ is a polyhedron then we can apply Lemma 6 to get a stronger condition to enforce the constraint on P^j, P^k, q^j, q^k and r^j, r^k of Eq. (12) and we obtain:

$$\forall \, x \in X^i \cap S^j \cap (f^i)^{-1}(S^k),$$
$$r^j + 2 x^\mathsf{T} q^j + x^\mathsf{T} P^j x - f^i(x)^\mathsf{T} P^k f^i(x) - 2 f^i(x)^\mathsf{T} q^k - r^k \geq 0. \quad (13)$$

In Eq. (13), we use Lemma 6 with the positive scalar λ equal to 1 to avoid to introduce a bilinear constraint. In Eq. (13), we recognize a positivity constraint of a quadratic form on a polyhedron and thus can be reinforced by a stronger constraint involving cone-copositive matrices. Finally the constraint for all $i \in \mathcal{I}$, $f^i \left(X^i \cap S^{\text{ind}} \right) \subseteq S^{\text{ind}}$ is replaced by the stronger condition:

$$\forall \, i \in \mathcal{I}, \; \forall \, (j,k) \in [n]^2 \text{ s.t. } (i,j,k) \in \text{Com}(\mathcal{X}, \mathcal{S}, f^{i^{-1}}(\mathcal{S})),$$
$$\mathbf{M}(P^j, 2q^j, r^j) - F^i \mathbf{M}(P^k, 2q^k, r^k) F^i \in \mathbf{C}_{d+1} \left(\mathbf{H} \left(X^i \cap S^j \cap (f^i)^{-1}(S^k) \right) \right) \quad (14)$$

3.3 Optimality

We detail how to evaluate $\sup_{x \in S^{\text{ind}}} x^\mathsf{T} M x + 2 p^\mathsf{T} x$. First, since:

$$\sup_{x \in S^{\text{ind}}} x^\mathsf{T} M x + 2 p^\mathsf{T} x = \inf \{\eta \mid \eta - x^\mathsf{T} M x - 2 p^\mathsf{T} x \geq 0, \; \forall \, x \in S^{\text{ind}}\}$$

Now $\eta - x^\mathsf{T} M x - 2 p^\mathsf{T} x \geq 0$, $\forall \, x \in S^{\text{ind}}$ is equivalent to say that for all $i \in [n]$, we have $\eta - x^\mathsf{T} M x - 2 p^\mathsf{T} x \geq 0$ for all $x \in S^i \cap \{y \in \mathbb{R}^d \mid y^\mathsf{T} P^i y + 2 y^\mathsf{T} q^i + r^i \leq 0\}$. Since $x^\mathsf{T} P^i x + 2 x^\mathsf{T} q^i + r^i \leq 0$ is a quadratic constraint and S^i is a polyhedron then we can apply Lemma 6. Finally $\eta - x^\mathsf{T} M x - 2 p^\mathsf{T} x \geq 0$, $\forall \, x \in S^{\text{ind}}$ is replaced by the stronger constraint:

$$\mathbf{M}(P^i, 2q^i, r^i) - \mathbf{M}(M, 2p, -\eta) \in \mathbf{C}_{d+1} \left(\mathbf{H} \left(S^i \right) \right) \quad (15)$$

Theorem 1 (Optimality). *Assume there exists $\{(P^i, q^i, r^i), P^i \in \mathbb{S}_d, q^i \in \mathbb{R}^d, \; i \in [n]\}$, a polyhedric partition $\mathcal{S} = (S^1, \ldots, S^n)$ and a real η such that Eqs. (11), (14) and (15) hold. Recall that $S^{\text{ind}} = \cup_{i \in [n]} \{x \in S^i \mid x^\mathsf{T} P^i x + 2 x^\mathsf{T} q^i + r^i \leq 0\}$. Then, $\mathcal{R} \subseteq S^{\text{ind}} \subseteq \{x \in \mathbb{R}^d \mid x^\mathsf{T} M x + 2 x^\mathsf{T} p \leq \eta\}$.*

3.4 Implementable Model Using Semidefinite Programming

Finally, we construct a model using semidefinite programming. First, we choose as polyhedric partition the one of the system i.e. $\mathcal{S} = \mathcal{X}$. Second, as said before, we use Corollary 2 to rewrite copositive constraints as semidefinite ones. Then Eq. (11) becomes:

$$\forall\, i \in \mathrm{Com}(\{X^{\mathrm{in}}\}, \mathcal{X}),$$
$$\mathbf{M}(-P^i, -2q^i, -r^i) - \mathbf{H}\left(X^{\mathrm{in}} \cap X^i\right)^{\mathsf{T}} \left(Z_p^i + Z_+^i\right) \mathbf{H}\left(X^{\mathrm{in}} \cap X^i\right) \succeq 0 \quad (16)$$

where Z_p^i are unknown matrices with nonnegative coefficients and Z_+^i are unknown positive semidefinite matrices. Since $\mathcal{S} = \mathcal{X}$, then $X^i \cap S^j$ in Eq. (14) is replaced by X^i and Eq. (14) becomes:

$$\forall\, i \in \mathcal{I},\ \forall\, k \in \mathcal{I}\ \text{s.t.}\ (i, k) \in \mathrm{Com}(\mathcal{X}, f^{i^{-1}}(\mathcal{X}))$$
$$\mathbf{M}(P^i, 2q^i, r^i) - F^{i^{\mathsf{T}}}\mathbf{M}(P^k, 2q^k, r^k)F^i$$
$$-\mathbf{H}\left(X^i \cap (f^i)^{-1}(X^k)\right)^{\mathsf{T}} \left(U_p^{ik} + U_+^{ik}\right) \mathbf{H}\left(X^i \cap (f^i)^{-1}(X^k)\right) \succeq 0\,; \quad (17)$$

where U_p^{ik} are unknown matrices with nonnegative coefficients and U_+^{ik} are unknown positive semidefinite matrices. Equation (15) becomes:

$$\forall\, i \in \mathcal{I},\ \mathbf{M}(P^i, 2q^i, r^i) - \mathbf{M}(M, 2p, -\eta) - \mathbf{H}\left(X^i\right)^{\mathsf{T}} \left(W_p^i + W_+^i\right) \mathbf{H}\left(X^i\right) \succeq 0 \quad (18)$$

where W_p^i are unknown matrices with nonnegative coefficients and W_+^i are unknown positive semidefinite matrices. Let us introduce the following families:

- $\mathcal{P} := \{(P^i, q^i, r^i), P^i \in \mathbb{S}_d, q^i \in \mathbb{R}^d,\ i \in \mathcal{I}\}$
- $\mathcal{W} := \{\left(W_p^i, W_+^i\right) \in \mathbb{S}_{n_i+1}^{\geq 0} \times \mathbb{S}_{n_i+1}^+, i \in \mathcal{I}\}$,
- $\mathcal{U} := \{\left(U_p^{ij}, U_+^{ij}\right) \in \mathbb{S}_{n_{ik}}^{\geq 0} \times \mathbb{S}_{n_{ik}}^+, (i, k) \in \mathrm{Com}(\mathcal{X}, f^{i^{-1}}(\mathcal{X}))\}$
- $\mathcal{Z} := \{\left(Z_p^{i0}, Z_+^{i0}\right) \in \mathbb{S}_{n_{i0}}^{\geq 0} \times \mathbb{S}_{n_{i0}}^+, i \in \mathrm{Com}(\{X^{\mathrm{in}}\}, \mathcal{X})\}$

The integers $n_i + 1$ are the sizes of the matrices $\mathbf{H}\left(X^i\right)$, n_{ik} the sizes of the matrices $\mathbf{H}\left(X^i \cap (f^i)^{-1}(X^k)\right)$ and n_{i0} the sizes of the matrices $\mathbf{H}\left(X^{\mathrm{in}} \cap X^i\right)$.

Let us consider the problem:

$$\inf_{\substack{\mathcal{P}, \mathcal{W}, \mathcal{U}, \mathcal{Z}, \\ \alpha, \beta}} -\sum_i r^i + \eta$$
$$\text{s.t.} \quad \begin{cases} (\mathcal{P}, \mathcal{W}, \mathcal{U}, \mathcal{Z}, \eta) \text{ satisfies (18), (17) and (16)} \\ \forall\, i \in \mathcal{I},\ r^i \leq 0,\ \eta \in \mathbb{R} \end{cases} \qquad \text{(PSD)}$$

Problem (PSD) is thus a semi-definite program. The use of the sum $-\sum_i r^i + \eta$ as objective function enforces the functions $x \mapsto x^{\mathsf{T}}P^i x + 2x^{\mathsf{T}}q^i + r^i$ to provide a minimal bound η and a minimal ellipsoid containing the initial conditions. However, $r^i \leq 0$ is not natural but ensures that the objective function is bounded from below. The presence of the constraint $r^i \leq 0$ does not affect the feasibility. Note that to reduce the size of the problem, we can take $q^i = 0$ and get homogeneous functions.

3.5   Results on Example 1

Boundedness Property. Recall the running example which consists of the following PWA: $X^{\text{in}} = [-1, 1] \times [-1, 1]$, and, for all $k \in \mathbb{N}$:

$$x_{k+1} = \begin{cases} A^1 x_k & \text{if } x_{k,1} \geq 0 \text{ and } x_{k,2} \geq 0 \\ A^2 x_k & \text{if } x_{k,1} \geq 0 \text{ and } x_{k,2} < 0 \\ A^3 x_k & \text{if } x_{k,1} < 0 \text{ and } x_{k,2} < 0 \\ A^4 x_k & \text{if } x_{k,1} < 0 \text{ and } x_{k,2} \geq 0 \end{cases}$$

with

$$A^1 = \begin{pmatrix} -0.04 & -0.461 \\ -0.139 & 0.341 \end{pmatrix}, \quad A^2 = \begin{pmatrix} 0.936 & 0.323 \\ 0.788 & -0.049 \end{pmatrix}$$

$$A^3 = \begin{pmatrix} -0.857 & 0.815 \\ 0.491 & 0.62 \end{pmatrix}, \quad A^4 = \begin{pmatrix} -0.022 & 0.644 \\ 0.758 & 0.271 \end{pmatrix}$$

Then, we have $X^1 = \mathbb{R}_+ \times \mathbb{R}_+$, $X^2 = \mathbb{R}_+ \times \mathbb{R}_-^*$, $X^3 = \mathbb{R}_-^* \times \mathbb{R}_-^*$ and $X^4 = \mathbb{R}_-^* \times \mathbb{R}_+$. Hence, $\mathcal{X} = \{X^1, X^2, X^3, X^4\}$. We write $f^{-1}(\mathcal{X})$ for the union of the polyhedric partitions $(f^i)^{-1}(\mathcal{X})$.

We are interested in proving the boundedness of the reachable values set of the PWA. Then, we have to solve the optimization problem:

$$\sup_{(x_1, x_2) \in \mathcal{R}} \|(x_1, x_2)\|_2^2$$

To get an overapproximation of the optimal value $\sup_{(x_1, x_2) \in \mathcal{R}} \|(x_1, x_2)\|_2^2$ we solve Problem (PSD). Before it, we have to compute the two sets of indices $\text{Com}(\{X^{\text{in}}\}, \mathcal{X})$ and $\text{Com}(\mathcal{X}, f^{-1}(\mathcal{X}))$. From Corollary 1, we computed using linear programming $\text{Com}(\{X^{\text{in}}\}, \mathcal{X}) = \{1, 2, 3, 4\}$ and $\text{Com}(\mathcal{X}, f^{-1}(\mathcal{X})) = \{(i, j) \mid S(i, j) = 1\}$ with $S = \begin{pmatrix} 1 & 0 & 1 & 1 \\ 1 & 0 & 0 & 1 \\ 0 & 1 & 1 & 0 \\ 1 & 1 & 0 & 0 \end{pmatrix}$.

Now by solving Problem (PSD), we get a (optimal) piecewise quadratic function V^{ind} characterized by the following matrices:

$$P^1 = \begin{pmatrix} 1.1178 & -0.1178 \\ -0.1178 & 1.1178 \end{pmatrix}, \quad P^2 = \begin{pmatrix} 1.5907 & 0.5907 \\ 0.5907 & 1.5907 \end{pmatrix},$$

$$P^3 = \begin{pmatrix} 1.3309 & -0.3309 \\ -0.3309 & 1.3309 \end{pmatrix}, \quad P^4 = \begin{pmatrix} 1.2558 & 0.2558 \\ 0.2558 & 1.2558 \end{pmatrix}$$

The vectors q^1, q^2 q^3 and q^4 are equal to the null vector. Since $r^1 = r^2 = r^3 = r^4 = -2$ and $\eta = 2$, then $\mathcal{R} \subseteq \cup_{i \in \{1,2,3,4\}} \{x \in X^i \mid x^{\mathsf{T}} P^i x \leq 2\} \subseteq \{x \in \mathbb{R}^2 \mid \|x\|_2^2 \leq 2\}$. The sets $\mathcal{R}$ (a discretized version of it) and $\{x \in \mathbb{R}^2 \mid V^{\text{ind}}(x) \leq 2\}$ are depicted at Fig. 2.

Optimal Value for the First Coordinate. We still consider the running example Example 1 but now, we are interested in the first coordinate. Thus, we consider the following optimization problem: $\sup_{(x_1, x_2) \in \mathcal{R}} x_1^2$. Now by solving

Problem (PSD), we get a (optimal) PQL function V^{ind} characterized by the following matrices:

$$P^1 = \begin{pmatrix} 1.0585 & -0.1169 \\ -0.1169 & 0.2339 \end{pmatrix}, \quad P^2 = \begin{pmatrix} 1.0276 & 0.0553 \\ 0.0553 & 0.1105 \end{pmatrix},$$

$$P^3 = \begin{pmatrix} 1.1739 & -0.3478 \\ -0.3478 & 0.6956 \end{pmatrix}, \quad P^4 = \begin{pmatrix} 1.1220 & 0.2440 \\ 0.2440 & 0.4880 \end{pmatrix}$$

For this problem, the vectors q^1, q^2 q^3 and q^4 are equal to the null vector and $r^1 = -1.0585$, $r^2 = -1.0276$, $r^3 = -1.1739$ and $r^4 = -1.122$ and $\eta = 1.1739$. Then, the optimal value $\sup_{(x_1,x_2)\in\mathcal{R}} x_1^2 \leq 1.1739$. Moreover, it seems that the maximum is reached in the cell X^3.

Optimal Value for the Second Coordinate. We again consider the running example Example 1 and we consider the values taken by the second coordinate. Thus, we consider the following optimization problem: $\sup_{(x_1,x_2)\in\mathcal{R}} x_2^2$. Now by solving Problem (PSD), we get a (optimal) PQL function V^{ind} characterized by the following matrices:

$$P^1 = \begin{pmatrix} 0.0198 & -0.0099 \\ -0.0099 & 1.0050 \end{pmatrix}, \quad P^2 = \begin{pmatrix} 0.6919 & 0.2292 \\ 0.2292 & 1.0759 \end{pmatrix},$$

$$P^3 = \begin{pmatrix} 0.5746 & -0.1706 \\ -0.1706 & 1.0759 \end{pmatrix}, \quad P^4 = \begin{pmatrix} 0.6109 & 0.3054 \\ 0.3054 & 1.1527 \end{pmatrix}$$

For this problem, the vectors q^1, q^2 q^3 and q^4 are equal to the null vector and $r^1 = -1.0050$, $r^2 = -1.3094$, $r^3 = -1.3094$ and $r^4 = -1.1527$ and $\eta = 1.3094$. Then, the optimal value $\sup_{(x_1,x_2)\in\mathcal{R}} x_2^2 \leq 1.3094$. Moreover, it seems that the maximum is reached in the cell X^3 and in the cell X^4.

A random property. Let us prove that the reachable value set is fully contained in the ellipsoid $\{(x,y) \in \mathbb{R}^2 \mid -x^2 + 2y^2 - xy + x - 0.5y \leq 6\}$. Thus, we consider the following optimization problem: $\sup_{(x_1,x_2)\in\mathcal{R}} -x^2 + 2y^2 - xy + x - 0.5y$. Now by solving Problem (PSD), we get a (optimal) PQL function V^{ind} characterized by the following matrices:

$$P^1 = \begin{pmatrix} 0.4226 & -0.8129 \\ -0.8129 & 2.0688 \end{pmatrix}, \quad P^2 = \begin{pmatrix} 0.4558 & -0.1418 \\ -0.1418 & 2.4936 \end{pmatrix},$$

$$P^3 = \begin{pmatrix} 1.9959 & -0.5084 \\ -0.5084 & 2.1136 \end{pmatrix}, \quad P^4 = \begin{pmatrix} 1.4772 & 0.7386 \\ 0.7386 & 2.6193 \end{pmatrix}$$

For this problem, the vectors q^1, q^2 q^3 and q^4 are equal to the null vector and $r^1 = -2.0688$, $r^2 = -3.2331$, $r^3 = -3.0927$ and $r^4 = -2.6193$ and $\eta = 5.2936$. Then, the optimal value $\sup_{(x_1,x_2)\in\mathcal{R}} -x^2 + 2y^2 - xy + x - 0.5y \leq 5.2936$. This results validates the property.

4 Conclusion and Future Works

The paper presents an implementable method to prove automatically that the reachable values set of a PWA is contained in an ellipsoid. In this case, to check the property is equivalent to solve a maximization problem. The constraint of this maximization problem is formulated as to belong to the reachable values set of the analyzed PWA. By using abstraction by union of truncated ellipsoids, we get an overapproximation of the optimal value of the problem. The method developed in the paper uses a semidefinite relaxation of copositive constraints.

First, we plan to complete the benchmarks: to apply the method for more non-trivial properties such that the avoidance of unsafe regions or "viability" properties. Some easy extensions can be done such as the consideration of union of truncated ellipsoids as property set representations instead of ellipsoids. An extension to constrained piecewise affine systems i.e. with a stopping condition on the system can be easily considered.

References

1. Adjé, A., Garoche, P.-L.: Automatic synthesis of piecewise linear quadratic invariants for programs. In: D'Souza, D., Lal, A., Larsen, K.G. (eds.) VMCAI 2015. LNCS, vol. 8931, pp. 99–116. Springer, Heidelberg (2015). doi:10.1007/978-3-662-46081-8_6
2. Adjé, A., Garoche, P.-L., Magron, V.: Property-based polynomial invariant generation using sums-of-squares optimization. In: Blazy, S., Jensen, T. (eds.) SAS 2015. LNCS, vol. 9291, pp. 235–251. Springer, Heidelberg (2015). doi:10.1007/978-3-662-48288-9_14
3. Allamigeon, X.: Static analysis of memory manipulations by abstract interpretation – Algorithmics of tropical polyhedra, and application to abstract interpretation. Ph.D. thesis, École Polytechnique, Palaiseau, France, November 2009
4. Allamigeon, X., Gaubert, S., Goubault, E., Putot, S., Stott, N.: A scalable algebraic method to infer quadratic invariants of switched systems. In: 2015 International Conference on Embedded Software, EMSOFT 2015, Amsterdam, Netherlands, October 4–9, 2015, pp. 75–84 (2015)
5. Bomze, I.M., Schachinger, W., Uchida, G.: Think co(mpletely)positive ! matrix properties, examples and a clustered bibliography on copositive optimization. J. Glob. Optim. 52(3), 423–445 (2012)
6. Bundfuss, S., Dür, M.: An adaptive linear approximation algorithm for copositive programs. SIAM J. Optim. 20(1), 30–53 (2009)
7. Cousot, P., Cousot, R.: Abstract interpretation: a unified lattice model for static analysis of programs by construction or approximation of fixpoints. In: Conference Record of the Fourth Annual ACM SIGPLAN-SIGACT Symposium on Principles of Programming Languages, pp. 238–252. Los Angeles, California, NY (1977)
8. Diananda, P.H.: On non-negative forms in real variables some or all of which are non-negative. Math. Proc. Camb. Philos. Soc. 58(1), 17–25 (1962)
9. Johansson, M.: On modeling, analysis and design of piecewise linear control systems. In: Proceedings of the 2003 International Symposium on Circuits and Systems, 2003. ISCAS 2003, vol. 3, pp. III-646–III-649 (2003)

10. Martin, D.H., Jacobson, D.H.: Copositive matrices and definiteness of quadratic forms subject to homogeneous linear inequality constraints. Linear Algebra Appl. **35**, 227–258 (1981)
11. Maxfield, J.E., Minc, H.: On the matrix equation X'X = A. Proc. Edinb. Math. Soc. (Series 2) **13**(12), 125–129 (1962)
12. Mignone, D., Ferrari-Trecate, G., Morari, M.: Stability and stabilization of piecewise affine and hybrid systems: an lmi approach. In: Proceedings of the 39th IEEE Conference on Decision and Control, vol. 1, pp. 504–509 (2000)
13. Motzkin, T.S.: Two consequences of the transposition theorem on linear inequalities. Econometrica **19**(2), 184–185 (1951)

Formal Analysis of Engineering Systems Based on Signal-Flow-Graph Theory

Sidi Mohamed Beillahi[(✉)], Umair Siddique, and Sofiène Tahar

Department of Electrical and Computer Engineering,
Concordia University, Montreal, QC, Canada
{beillahi,muh_sidd,tahar}@ece.concordia.ca

Abstract. Signal-flow-graph theory provides an efficient framework to model various engineering and physical systems at a higher-level of abstraction. In this paper, we present the formalization of the signal-flow-graph theory with an ultimate goal to conduct the formal analysis of engineering systems within a higher-order-logic theorem prover. In particular, our formalization can tackle system models which are based on undirected graphs. We also present the formalization of the system transfer function and associated properties such as stability and resonance. In order to demonstrate the effectiveness of our work, we present the formal analysis of two engineering systems namely the PANDA Vernier resonator and the z-source impedance network, which are commonly used in photonics and power electronics, respectively.

1 Introduction

A signal-flow-graph (SFG) [17] is a diagram that represents a set of simultaneous linear algebraic equations describing the flow of different physical quantities (e.g., electric current) from one point of the system to another point. Many physical and engineering systems ranging from analog circuits to photonic signal processors can be represented using the signal-flow-graph theory. Generally, there are two types of SFGs, i.e., directed and undirected [23,24]. In a directed SFG, nodes should be ordered, whereas an undirected SFG does not require a strict ordering of nodes which makes it more convenient to model a variety of systems such as photonic filters and analog power converters.

Once an SFG representation of the underlying system has been built, the next step is to analyze the corresponding behavior to ensure that the system meets its specification. The Mason's Gain Formula (MGF) [15,16] provides an efficient way to obtain a transfer function (input-output relation) directly from the SFG representation. Moreover, the obtained transfer function is used to investigate different properties of the system such as stability (which ensures that the output is bounded whenever the input in bounded). Some of the main applications of MGF include the analysis of wireless networks [14], security protocols [7], process engineering [13], power electronics [12,20] and photonic signal processing [5].

In the past few decades, formal methods [6] have been successfully applied to improve the analysis of a variety of software, hardware and physical systems.

© Springer International Publishing AG 2017
S. Bogomolov et al. (Eds.): NSV 2016, LNCS 10152, pp. 31–46, 2017.
DOI: 10.1007/978-3-319-54292-8_3

The main idea behind formal analysis of a system is to construct a computer based mathematical model of the given system and formally check that the model meets its specifications. The rigorous process of building a mathematical model for the given system and analyzing this model using mathematical reasoning usually increases the chances for catching subtle but critical design errors that are often ignored by traditional techniques such as paper-and-pencil based proofs, numerical methods or simulation. Given the extensive usage of signal-flow-graph to model engineering systems that are employed in safety-critical applications, we believe that there is a dire need of building a formal framework to reason about the signal-flow-graph theory.

The involvement of complex-valued parameters requires an expressive technique to formalize the notions of the signal-flow-graph theory and MGF. Higher-order-logic (HOL) theorem proving [11] is a generic formal methods technique which provides such an expressive formalism to reason about multivariate analysis. In [4], we used the HOL Light theorem prover to formalize the notion of signal-flow-graph theory and the procedure to obtain the transfer function for directed SFGs based on MGF. We applied this formalization to verify the stability of power electronic converters. However, this formalization can only be used for directed SFGs which limits its usage for many practical systems. In this paper, we build upon our previous work and formalize undirected SFG theory and MGF along with the notion of system stability. We apply this formalization to two distinct domains, i.e., power electronics and photonics. Indeed, we present in this paper the formal verification of z-source impedance network [10] and PANDA Vernier resonator [1] which are commonly used systems in power electronics and photonics, respectively. The source code of our formalization is available for download [2] and can be utilized by other researchers and engineers for further developments and the analysis of more practical systems.

The rest of the paper is organized as follows: we give a preliminary review of the SFG theory and the Mason's Gain Formula in Sect. 2. We present the HOL formalization of undirected SFGs in Sect. 3. Consequently, in Sect. 4, we provide the formalization of transfer functions along with the notion of stability and resonance. We describe the formal analysis of the z-source impedance network and PANDA Vernier resonator as illustrative practical applications in Sects. 5 and 6, respectively. Finally, Sect. 7 concludes the paper and provides hints for some future directions.

2   Signal-Flow Graphs Theory and Mason's Gain Formula

Mathematically, a signal-flow-graph represents a set of linear algebraic equations of the corresponding system [16]. An SFG is a network in which nodes are connected by directed branches. Every node in the network represents a system variable and each branch represents the signal transmission from one node to the other under the assumption that signals flow only in one direction. An example of an SFG is shown in Fig. 1 consisting of six nodes. An input or *source node* and an output or *sink node* are usually the ones which only have outgoing branches and incoming branches, respectively (e.g., nodes 1 and 6 in Fig. 1). A branch is a directed line from node i to j and the gain of each branch is called the *transmittance*. A *path* is a traversal of connected branches from one node to the other and if no node is crossed more than once and connects the input to the output, then the path is called *forward path*, otherwise if it leads back to itself without crossing any node more than once, it is considered as a *closed path* or a *loop*. A loop containing only one node is called a *self loop* and any two loops in the SFG are said to be *touching loops* if they have any common node. The total gain of a forward path and a loop can be computed by multiplying the transmittances of each traversed branch. In the analysis of practical engineering systems (resp. process), the main task is to characterize the relation among the system's (resp. process) input and output which is called the transfer function. The total transmittance or gain between two given nodes (usually input and output) describes the transfer function of the corresponding system. In 1953, Mason [16] proposed a computational procedure (also called Mason's Gain Formula) to obtain the total gain of any arbitrary signal-flow-graph. The formula is described in Eq. 1 as follows:

$$G = \sum_k \frac{G_k \Delta_k}{\Delta} \tag{1}$$

$$\Delta = 1 - \sum_m P_{m1} + \sum_m P_{m2} - \sum_m P_{m3} + \ldots + (-1)^n \sum \ldots \tag{2}$$

where Δ represents the determinant of the graph, Δ_k represents the value of Δ for the part of the graph that is not touching the kth forward path and it is called the cofactor of forward path k, P_{mr} is the gain product of mth possible combination of r non-touching loops. The gain of each forward path is represented by G_k.

For example, in Fig. 1 taking the nodes 1 and 6 as the input and output nodes, respectively. There is one forward path ($1 \rightarrow 2 \rightarrow 3 \rightarrow 4 \rightarrow 5 \rightarrow 6$) and

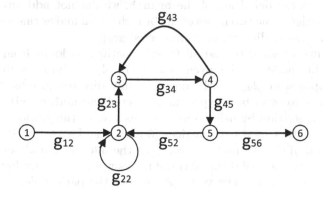

Fig. 1. A signal-flow graph

three loops ($2 \to 2$, $2 \to 3 \to 4 \to 5 \to 2$ and $3 \to 4 \to 3$). Thus, we can find the input to output transfer function using the MGF as follows:

$$G = \frac{g_{12} \cdot g_{23} \cdot g_{34} \cdot g_{45} \cdot g_{56}}{1 - g_{22} - g_{23} \cdot g_{34} \cdot g_{45} \cdot g_{52} - g_{34} \cdot g_{43} + g_{22} \cdot g_{34} \cdot g_{43}} \qquad (3)$$

3   Formalization of Undirected Signal-Flow-Graph Theory

We model a single branch as a triplet (a, t_{ab}, b), where a, t_{ab} and b represent the start node, the transmittance and the end node, respectively. Consequently, a path can be modeled as a list of branches and furthermore an SFG can be defined as a composition of paths along with the information about the total number of nodes in the circuit, the source and the sink nodes at which we want to compute the transfer function. As mentioned before, nodes and transmittance represent the system variables and gain, respectively. These parameters are indeed complex valued, i.e., $a, t_{ab}, c \in \mathbb{C}$ in the general context of engineering and physical systems. However, the information about the nodes is just used to find properties of signals (current) transmission and they do not appear in the gain and transfer function computation. So, we adapted the conventional approach as in [16], where nodes of an SFG are represented by natural numbers ($\mathbb{N}$). In order to simplify the reasoning process, we encode the above information by defining three type abbreviations in HOL Light[1], i.e., branch, path and signal-flow-graph as follows:

Definition 1 (Branch, Path and SFG).

```
new_type_abbrev ("branch", ':N × C × N')
new_type_abbrev ("path", ':(branch)list')
new_type_abbrev ("sfg", ':path × N × N × N')
```

where the second, third, and fourth elements of **sfg** represent the size, the output node and the input node of a signal-flow graphs, respectively. It is important to notice that in the definition of the **branch**, we did not add any constraint regarding the order of the two nodes of the branch which makes this formalization valid for both cases of directed and undirected graphs.

Our next main task is to find all forward paths and loops from the source node to the sink node for the given system. In [4], we implemented a search algorithm proposed in [24], which considers only directed graphs. In order to extend this work to cover both types (i.e., directed and undirected) of SFGs, we enhanced this algorithm by using some new features of the graph.

In [24], the author used two matrices (G and H) and a vector (P) to perform the search in an SFG. The matrix G contains the information about the graph, in particular, each row i of G contains the nodes where there are branches from i that end at these nodes. The vector P contains the path under consideration

---

[1] In this paper, we use minimal HOL Light syntax in the presentation of definitions and theorems to improve the readability.

in the search process, where the first element in the vector is the head of the path from which the search begins to construct the path. The matrix H is to ensure that we do not extract the same path twice. Each row i in the matrix H contains the nodes that cannot form a path with i (dead nodes). The procedure for extracting the loops can be subdivided into five steps as follows:

1. We first extract the graph information inside the matrix G and initialize the matrix H to 0. Then we initialize the elements of the vector P to 0 except the first element (which we initialize to 1) from which the search will start.
2. In the second step, we have a node i which is the tail of the vector P and we search for a node j in the graph that satisfies three conditions: (a) j is not in P (i.e., j is not already part of the path); (b) j is not in H(i) (i.e., j is not a dead node for i); (c) j >i (i.e., all paths are directed). The last condition constraints the application of this procedure on undirected SFGs. If j is found we add it in the vector P and repeat the process by replacing i by j. Finally, if no j is found, we stop the search and move to the next step.
3. In the third step, we want to confirm that the found path in the previous step is indeed a loop. If a loop is found, we report it and in all cases we go to the next step.
4. In this step, we confirm that an exhaustive search has been performed for all the loops that can start from the head of the vector P, otherwise, we initialize the row of H that contains all the dead nodes to the last node of vector P.
5. In this step, we check if the head of the vector P is the last node in the graph which indicates the termination of the search, otherwise, we replace the head of the vector P by the next node in the graph and we go back to the second step.

Note that the above procedure with slight modifications can be used for the forward path extraction. In order to extend this algorithm for undirected SFGs, we add two new matrices G_1 and H_1. The matrix G_1 contains some extra information about the graph where each row i contains the nodes where there are branches that start from these nodes and end at i. In graph theory, any element of a loop can be the head of the loop. Therefore, for computing loops this means that if we once did exhaustive search for all the loops that start from a certain node i then in the search for loops that start from another node j we do not need to consider the node i. This means i is a dead node for j. Hence, the matrix H_1 keeps track of these new dead nodes. The corresponding changes in the Steps 2 and 5 are summarized as follows:

- We change the third condition for extending the search and replace it by checking if j is not in $H_1(i)$ (means j is not a dead node for i).
- We add a new procedure by inserting the head of P in all the rows i of H_1 if there is a branch that starts from node i and ends at the head of P.

We next provide the definitions of two crucial functions in our formalization of undirected SFG that perform the Steps 2 and 5. The complete HOL formalization of the SFG theory can be found at [2].

Definition 2 (Next Node Search).

⊢ ∀(n m ∈ ℕ) (t1 t2 l1 l2 h1 ∈ ℕ list).
EC_next_node n m [] t2 l1 l2 h1 = 0 ∧
EC_next_node n (m + 1) (e1::t1) (e2::t2) l1 l2 h1 =
EC_next_node n m (e1::t1) t2 l1 l2 h1 ∧
EC_next_node n 0 (e1::t1) (e2::t2) l1 l2 h1 =
if ((NOT_IN_LIST e1 l1) ∧ (NOT_IN_LIST e1 l2) ∧ (NOT_IN_LIST e1 h1))
then n + 1 else EC_next_node (n + 1) 0 t1 (e2::t2) l1 l2 h1

where the vector P, the row H(i), and the row H_1(i) are represented as the lists l1, l2, h1, respectively. The function NOT_IN_LIST accepts a list and an element and tests the membership of the element. The main function EC_next_node returns (n + 1), which represents the position of the node e1 inside the list G[k] (list t1 in the definition) that satisfies the three conditions in Step 2, where k is the termination node for the considered path. In the process of searching for a path all the graph nodes are considered.

Next, we define the procedure to update the matrix H_1 after completing the search for loops that start from a given node e1. Here, e1 will be a dead node for all nodes for which branches exist that end at e1:

Definition 3 (Updating the Matrix H_1).

⊢ ∀ (e1 : num) (H1 : (num list) list) (l : num list).
EC_H1_MODIFIED e1 H1 [] = H1 ∧
EC_H1_MODIFIED e1 H1 (h::l) =
EC_H1_MODIFIED e1 (EC_H1_REPLACE (EC_H_MODIFIED0 H1[h − 1] e1) (h − 1) H1) l

where EC_H_MODIFIED0 accepts an element e1 and a list l (i.e., H_1[h − 1]) and searches for the leftmost zero in the list l and replaces it by e1. The function EC_H1_REPLACE takes a list l (i.e., EC_H_MODIFIED0 H_1[h − 1] e1), an integer (h − 1) and the matrix then it replaces the row H_1[h − 1] by l inside the matrix H.

A transpose of an SFG can be obtained by inverting all the branches and swapping input and output. We formally define the inversion of branches as follows:

Definition 4 (Inverse of Graph Branches).

⊢ ∀ (l : path). SFG_INVERSE [] = [] ∧ SFG_INVERSE e :: l =
(lst_of_trpl e, snd_of_trpl e, fst_of_trpl e)::SFG_INVERSE l

Here fst_of_trpl, snd_of_trpl, and lst_of_trpl return the first, second, and last element of a given triple, respectively. Using this definition, we formalize the graph transposition as follows:

Definition 5 (Graph Transpose).

⊢ ∀ sfg. SFG_TRANSPOSE sfg =
  (SFG_INVERSE (fst_of_four sfg), snd_of_four sfg,
  lst_of_four sfg, thd_of_four sfg)

In the next section, we provide the formalization of transfer function, Mason's gain formula and some associated properties.

4   Formalization of Transfer Function

As described in Sect. 2, Meson's Gain Formula requires the list of all loops to find the graph determinant and the list of forward paths to compute the graph numerator. We provide in below the main definition in the transfer function formalization, however, the complete formalization can be found at [2].

Definition 6 (Mason's gain formula).

$$\vdash \forall \, (\texttt{system} : \texttt{sfg}). \, \texttt{Mason\_Gain system} = \frac{\texttt{PRODUCT\_FORWARD\_DELTA (EC system) (FC system)}}{\texttt{DETERMINANT (EC system)}}$$

where `Mason_Gain` accepts an SFG (i.e., `system`) and returns the Mason's gain as given in Eq. 1. Notice that the function `PRODUCT_FORWARD_DELTA` accepts the lists of loops and forward paths (computed in Sect. 3) in the graph and computes $\sum_{k \in \texttt{system}} G_k \Delta_k$, where G_k and Δ_k represent, respectively, the product of all forward path gains and the determinant of the kth forward path considering the elimination of all loops touching the kth forward path as described in Sect. 2. The function `DETERMINANT` takes the list of loops and produces the determinant of the graph as described in Eq. (2). Finally, we utilize the above formalization along with loops and forward paths extraction procedures to formalize the transfer function of a given engineering system as follows:

Definition 7 (System Transfer Function).

$$\vdash \forall \, \texttt{system}. \, \texttt{transfer\_function system} = \texttt{Mason\_Gain} \, (\lambda \texttt{s. system s})$$

where the function `transfer_function` accepts a `system` which has type $\mathbb{C} \rightarrow \texttt{sfg}$ and returns a complex ($\mathbb{C}$) number which represents the transfer function of the engineering system (i.e., `system`). Here "s" is a complex parameter of the given system.

The availability of the transfer function provides the facility to analyze the stability and resonance conditions for the given system. Mathematically, the stability and resonance are concerned with the identification of all the values of **s** for which the system transfer function becomes infinite and zero, respectively. In the control theory and signal processing literature, these values are called *system poles* and *system zeros* which can be computed by the denominator and numerator of the transfer function, respectively. Furthermore, all poles and zeros must be inside the unit circle which means that their complex norm should be less or equal to 1. We formalize the above mentioned informal description of the system properties in HOL as follows:

Definition 8 (System Poles).

$$\vdash \forall \, \texttt{system}. \, \texttt{poles system} = \{ \texttt{s} \mid \texttt{denominator (system s)} = 0 \}$$
$$\vdash \forall \, \texttt{system}. \, \texttt{zeros system} = \{ \texttt{s} \mid \texttt{numerator (system s)} = 0 \}$$

where the functions poles and zeros take the system as a parameter and return the set of poles and zeros, respectively. Next, we formalize the notion of stability and resonance as follows:

Definition 9 (System Stability and Resonance).

$\vdash \forall$ system. is_stable system $[p_0, ..., p_n] \Leftrightarrow$

$\qquad \forall p_i. \ p_i \in$ (poles system) $\wedge \parallel p_i \parallel \leq 1$

$\vdash \forall$ system. is_resonant system $[z_0, ..., z_n] \Leftrightarrow$

$\qquad \forall z_i. \ z_i \in$ (zeros system) $\wedge \parallel z_i \parallel \leq 1$

where the predicate is_stable accepts a signal-flow-graph model (i.e., system) and a list of poles $[p_0, ..., p_n]$ and verifies that each element p_i is indeed a pole of the system and its corresponding magnitude (i.e., norm of a complex number, $\parallel p_i \parallel$) is smaller or equal to 1. The predicate is_resonant is defined in a similar way by considering the list of zeros instead of the list of poles of the system. In the above formalization, p_i and z_i are continuous complex functions.

In the following sections, we present the formal analysis of two engineering systems namely z-source impedance network and PANDA Vernier resonator. It is important to notice that the SFG of the PANDA Vernier resonator is undirected (e.g., the branch between the nodes 10 and 5). Furthermore, the SFG of the z-source impedance network is directed, however, its transpose is undirected.

5 Z-Source Impedance Network

The z-source is an impedance-source power converter that is considered to be more efficient than other commonly used power converters [19]. In [18], the authors claimed that the model of z-source can be applied to almost all DC-to-AC, AC-to-DC, AC-to-AC, and AC-to-DC power conversions. Thus it has been used in hybrid electric vehicles with dual mode, i.e., as a boost converter and buck converter [8]. The topology of z-source is composed of two-port network that consists of a split-inductors L1 and L2 and capacitors C1 and C2 connected in X shape [18]. The circuit configuration of the z-source impedance network is shown in Fig. 2, and its associate signal-flow-graph is depicted in Fig. 3 [10]. We first formally define the z-source impedance network model as follows:

Definition 10 (Z-source Impedance Network Model).

$\vdash \forall$ G1 G2 DA DD G5 R L C s $\in \mathbb{C}$.

$\quad$ ZSOURCE_model G1 G2 DA DD G5 R L C s =

$[(1, G1, 4); (1, G2, 7); (2, DA, 4); (3, R.DA, 4); (3, -DA, 7); (4, 1, 5); (5, \frac{1}{L.s}, 6);$

$(6, G5, 4); (6, DD, 7); (6, 1, 9); (7, 1, 8); (8, 1, 9); (8, \frac{1}{C.s}, 11); (9, 1, 10); (11, DD, 4);$

$(11, 2, 12)]$

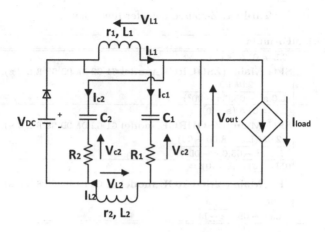

Fig. 2. Schematics of Z-source converter

where ZSOURCE_model represents the SFG of the z-source circuit depicted in Fig. 3 and it accepts the circuit parameters as the graph variables. We next formally verify the transfer function for the z-source impedance network between nodes 1 and 12 as follows:

Theorem 1 (Transfer Function of Z-source).

$\vdash\ \forall$ G1 G2 DA DD G5 R L C s $\in \mathbb{C}$. (C.L $\neq 0$) $\wedge$ (s $\neq 0$) $\implies$
transfer_function (ZSOURCE_model G1 G2 DA DD G5 R L C s, 12, 12, 1) =
$$\frac{2(\text{G2.L.s} + \text{G1.DD} - \text{G2.G5})}{\text{L.C.s}^2 - \text{G5.C.s} - \text{DD}^2}$$

where the two assumptions ensure that the gains $\frac{1}{\text{Ls}}$ and $\frac{1}{\text{Cs}}$ are well defined. The proof steps of the transfer function formula are mainly automated using a developed tactic that can be found at [2]. Similarly, we can derive other transfer functions which are listed in Table 1. Next, we present the formal verification of the stability conditions of the z-source impedance network under the global parameters:

Theorem 2 (Stability Conditions for Z-source).

$\vdash \forall$ G1 G2 DA DD G5 R L C $\in \mathbb{C}$.
$\left\| \frac{\text{G5.C} - \sqrt{(\text{G5.C})^2 + 4.(\text{L.C}).\text{DD}^2}}{2.\text{L.C}} \right\| \leq 1 \wedge \left\| \frac{\text{G5.C} + \sqrt{(\text{G5.C})^2 + 4.(\text{L.C}).\text{DD}^2}}{2.\text{L.C}} \right\| \leq 1 \wedge$

$\frac{\text{G5.C} + \sqrt{(\text{G5.C})^2 + 4.(\text{L.C}).\text{DD}^2}}{2.\text{L.C}} \neq 0 \wedge \text{C.L} \neq 0 \wedge \frac{\text{G5.C} - \sqrt{(\text{G5.C})^2 + 4.(\text{L.C}).\text{DD}^2}}{2.\text{L.C}} \neq 0 \implies$

is_stable (λ s. (ZSOURCE_model G1 G2 DA DD G5 R L C s, 12, 12, 1)) s

$\left[\frac{\text{G5.C} - \sqrt{(\text{G5.C})^2 + 4.(\text{L.C}).(\text{DD}^2)}}{2.\text{L.C}} ; \frac{\text{G5.C} + \sqrt{(\text{G5.C})^2 + 4.(\text{L.C}).(\text{DD}^2)}}{2.\text{L.C}} \right]$

Table 1. Z-source transfer functions

Transfer Function	Formula
$\dfrac{\hat{V}_{sum}}{\hat{V}_{dc}}$	$(\text{C.L} \neq 0) \wedge (\text{s} \neq 0) \Rightarrow$ $\textbf{SFG\_Main} ((\textbf{ZSOURCE\_model} \ \text{G1 G2 DA DD G5 R L C s}), 12, 12, 2) =$ $\dfrac{2.\text{DA.DD}}{(\text{L.C.s}^2 - \text{G5.C.s} - \text{DD}^2)}$
$\dfrac{\hat{V}_{sum}}{\hat{I}_{load}}$	$(\text{C.L} \neq 0) \wedge (\text{s} \neq 0) \Rightarrow$ $\textbf{SFG\_Main} ((\textbf{ZSOURCE\_model} \ \text{G1 G2 DA DD G5 R L C s}), 12, 12, 3) =$ $\dfrac{-2.\text{DA.}(\text{L.s} - \text{R.DD} - \text{G5})}{(\text{L.C.s}^2 - \text{G5.C.s} - \text{DD}^2)}$
$\dfrac{I_{in}}{\hat{V}_{dc}}$	$(\text{C.L} \neq 0) \wedge (\text{s} \neq 0) \Rightarrow$ $\textbf{SFG\_Main} ((\textbf{ZSOURCE\_model} \ \text{G1 G2 DA DD G5 R L C s}), 12, 10, 2) =$ $\dfrac{\text{DA.}(1 + \text{DD}).\text{C.s}}{\text{L.C.s}^2 - \text{G5.C.s} - \text{DD}^2}$

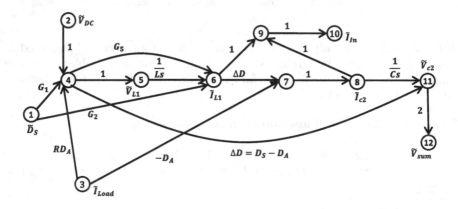

Fig. 3. Signal-flow-graph of Z-source converter

The first two assumptions ensure that both poles are inside the unit circle, whereas the last assumptions are required to prove that the poles are not equal to zero. Similarly, we verify the resonance condition for the z-source impedance network circuit as follows:

Theorem 3 (Resonance Conditions for Z-source).

$\vdash \forall$ G1 G2 DA DD G5 R L C $\in \mathbb{C}$.
    $\| \frac{\text{G2.G5}-\text{G1.DD}}{\text{G2.L}} \| \leq 1 \wedge \text{G2} \neq 0 \wedge (\text{G2.G5} - \text{G1.DD}) \neq 0 \wedge \text{C.L} \neq 0 \implies$
  is_resonant $(\lambda \ \text{s. } (\text{ZSOURCE\_model G1 G2 DA DD G5 R L C s}, 12, 12, 1))$ s
  $\left[\frac{\text{G2.G5}-\text{G1.DD}}{\text{G2.L}} \right]$

The assumptions in the theorem ensure that the system zero is inside the unit circle and it is not equal to zero. The proof steps for the two theorems are mainly based on first checking that the poles (resp. zeros) belong to the set of poles (resp.

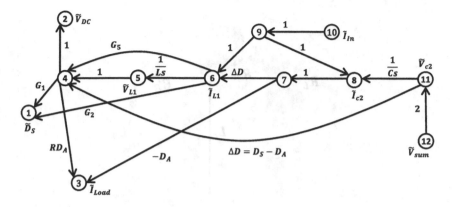

Fig. 4. Signal flow graph of Z-source converter transpose

zeros) defined in Definition 9. Then checking that the norm of these poles and zeros are less or equal to 1 using HOL rewriting rules. For electronic circuits, signal-flow-graph has a particular interesting feature, as shown in [20], namely, the transfer function of circuit transposition is the same as the original circuit. For example, Fig. 4 shows the transposed SFG of the z-source impedance network. We formally verified that the transfer functions of the z-source impedance network signal-flow-graph and its transpose (which is an *undirected* signal-flow-graph) are the same:

Theorem 4 (Transfer Function of Z-source Transpose).

$$\vdash \forall \; \texttt{G1 G2 DA DD G5 R L C s} \; \in \mathbb{C}. \quad (\texttt{C.L} \neq 0) \; \wedge \; (\texttt{s} \neq 0) \; \Longrightarrow$$
$$\texttt{transfer\_function (SFG\_TRANSPOSE (ZSOURCE\_model G1 G2 DA DD G5 R}$$
$$\texttt{L C s}, 12, 12, 1)) = \frac{2.(\texttt{G2.L.s} + \texttt{G1.DD} - \texttt{G2.G5})}{\texttt{L.C.s}^2 - \texttt{G5.C.s} - \texttt{DD}^2}$$

In the next section, we show another utilization of undirected SFG formalization to verify the transfer function of PANDA Vernier Resonator.

6   PANDA Vernier Resonator

The PANDA Vernier resonator is considered as a viable optical device for communication and signal processing [1,22]. It can also be employed as a force sensing application with a resolution in the range of micro-Newton. Figure 5 shows the configuration of the PANDA Vernier resonator where we have 4 optical directional couplers and 3 rings [1]. The directional couplers are optical devices that transfer the maximum possible optical power from one or more optical devices to another one in a selected direction. Optical rings are fiber rings that confine the light in a very small volume to perform different operations such as light amplification and wavelength filtering. Each coupler i is associated with

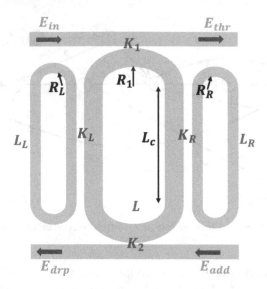

E_{in} K_1 E_{thr}

$R_L^{\updownarrow}$ $R_1^{\updownarrow}$ $R_R^{\updownarrow}$

L_L K_L L_c K_R L_R

L

K_2

E_{drp} E_{add}

Fig. 5. The PANDA resonator

the factor k_i ($i = 1, 2, r, l$) and the insertion loss γ. Consequently, the fraction of light passed through the through port of the coupler i is $C_i = \sqrt{(1-\gamma)(1-k_i)}$ and the fraction passed through the cross path is $S_i = \sqrt{(1-\gamma)k_i}$. Note that $C_i^2 + S_i^2 = 1 - \gamma \simeq 1$. Moreover, for each ring (i.e., main, right, and left) the parameter $e_i^p \equiv X_i Z^{-p}$ ($i = l, r$) is the multiplication of the one round-trip loss coefficient $X_i = exp(\frac{-\alpha L_i}{2})$ and the transmission of light $Z^{-p} = exp(-j\varphi p)$, where $\varphi = kn_{eff}L$ is the phase shift and p is the integer resonant mode numbers. The associated *undirected* SFG of PANDA resonator [1] is shown in Fig. 6. We formally define the PANDA Vernier resonator model as follows:

Definition 11 (PANDA Vernier Resonator Model).

$\vdash \forall$ er e el nr n nl sr s1 s2 sl cr c1 c2 cl $\in \mathbb{C}$.
  PANDA_model er e el nr n nl sr s1 s2 sl cr c1 c2 cl $=$
$[(1, c1, 3); (1, -j.s1, 4); (2, c1, 4); (2, -j.s1, 3); (4, \sqrt[4]{e^n}, 9); (9, cr, 10);$
$(9, -j.sr, 12); (12, \sqrt{er^{nr}}, 13); (13, \sqrt{er^{nr}}, 11); (11, -j.sr, 10); (11, cr, 12);$
$(10, \sqrt[4]{e^n}, 5); (5, c2, 7); (5, -j.s2, 8); (6, c2, 8); (6, -j.s2, 7); (7, \sqrt[4]{e^n}, 14);$
$(14, c1, 15); (14, -j.sl, 17); (17, \sqrt{el^{nl}}, 18); (18, \sqrt{el^{nl}}, 16); (16, c1, 17);$
$(16, -j.sl, 15); (15, \sqrt[4]{e^n}, 2)]$

Based on this definition, we formally prove the optical transfer function for the through port of the PANDA Vernier resonator between nodes 1 and 3, as follows:

Theorem 5 (Transfer Function of the through port).
$\vdash \forall$ er e el nr n nl sr s1 s2 sl cr c1 c2 cl $\in \mathbb{C}$.

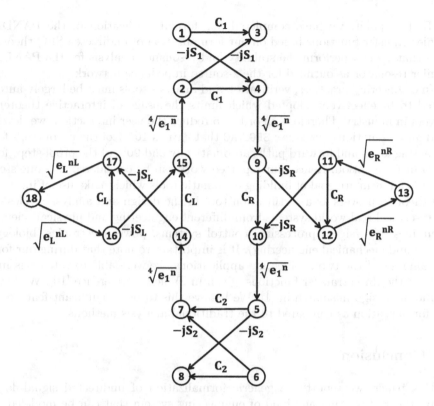

Fig. 6. Signal flow graph of the PANDA resonator

$$(c1^2 + s1^2) = 1 \wedge (c2^2 + s2^2) = 1 \wedge (cr^2 + sr^2) = 1 \wedge (cl^2 + sl^2) = 1 \implies$$

transfer_function (PANDA_model er e el nr n nl sr s1 s2 sl cr

c1 c2 cl, 18, 3, 1) = $\{c1.(1 + cl.cr.er^{nr}.el^{nl} - cl.el^{nl} - cr.er^{nr}) +$

$\qquad c2.e^n.(cl.er^{nr} + cr.el^{nl} - cr.cl - er^{nr}.e^{nl})\}$

$\{1 - cl.el^{nl} - cr.er^{nr} - cr.cl.c1.c2.e^n + cl.cr.er^{nr}.el^{nl} +$

$cl.c1.c2.er^{nr}.e^n + cr.c1.c2.el^{nl}.e^n - c1.c2.er^{nr}.el^{nl}.e^n\}$

We also formally verify the drop-port optical transfer function for the PANDA Vernier resonators between nodes 1 and 8, as follows:

Theorem 6 (Transfer Function of the drop-port).

$\vdash \forall$ er e el nr n nl sr s1 s2 sl cr c1 c2 cl $\in \mathbb{C}$.

$\quad (c1^2 + s1^2) = 1 \wedge (c2^2 + s2^2) = 1 \wedge (cr^2 + sr^2) = 1 \wedge (cl^2 + sl^2) = 1 \implies$

transfer_function (PANDA_model er e el nr n nl sr s1 s2 sl cr

c1 c2 cl, 18, 8, 1) = $\{s1.s2.er^{nr}.\sqrt{e^n} - s1.s2.cl.el^{nl}.er^{nr}.\sqrt{e^n} -$

$\qquad cr.s1.s2.\sqrt{e^n} + cr.cl.s1.s2.el^{nl}.\sqrt{e^n}\}$

$\{1 - cl.el^{nl} - cr.er^{nr} - cr.cl.c1.c2.e^n + cl.cr.er^{nr}.el^{nl} +$

$cl.c1.c2.er^{nr}.e^n + cr.c1.c2.el^{nl}.e^n - c1.c2.er^{nr}.el^{nl}.e^n\}$

To this point, we have completed our formal verification of the PANDA Vernier transfer functions based on our formalization of undirected SFG theory. Note that we can perform the stability and resonance analysis for the PANDA Vernier resonator as outlined for the z-source impedance network.

In engineering practices, verification and analysis tools must be largely automated to be effectively adopted which limits the usage of interactive theorem provers in industry. Therefore, in order to reduce the user interaction, we developed an automation procedure; SFG_TAC that carries 100% of the proof steps for extracting loops and forward paths automatically and 90% of the proof steps for the transfer function. Hence, our reported work can be considered as a one step towards an ultimate goal of building automatic tools which make use of interactive theorem provers as a certification tool in the design and analysis cycles of safety-critical real-world systems from different engineering and physical science disciplines (e.g., signal processing, control systems, power electronics, biology, optical and mechanical engineering). It is important to note that during our formal analysis of the two engineering applications, we were able to catch missing parts in the three transfer functions, given in Table 1 in reference [10]. We have also found a sign mismatch in [1]. We believe this to be a significant feature of our formalization as compared to the traditional analysis methods.

7   Conclusion

In this paper, we reported a generic formalization of undirected signal-flow-graph theory targeting any kind of engineering system that can be modeled in the form of a signal-flow-graph. We provided an overview of our formalization including the notion of loop extraction and the transposition of a signal-flow-graph. Consequently, we derive the transfer functions of two real-world engineering applications: (1) the PANDA Vernier resonator; and (2) the z-source impedance network. We described the formal analysis of the stability and resonance conditions for the z-source impedance network. Moreover, we formally verified that the z-source impedance network and its transpose have the same transfer function.

Our immediate future work is to develop upon the existing automation procedures to fully automate the proof process and to build a tool that makes use of these procedures for the analysis of engineering systems (e.g., photonics processors [21] and process engineering [3]). Another potential utilization of our formalization and developed automation tactics is to build a framework to certify the results produced by informal tools such as MATLAB based SFG analysis program (available at [9]).

References

1. Bahadoran, M., Ali, J., Yupapin, P.P.: Ultrafast all-optical switching using signal flow graph for PANDA resonator. Appl. Opt. **52**(12), 2866–2873 (2013)
2. Beillahi, S.M., Siddique, U.: Formal analysis of engineering systems based on signal-flow-graph theory (2016). http://hvg.ece.concordia.ca/projects/control/sfg.html
3. Beillahi, S.M., Siddique, U., Tahar, S.: Towards the application of formal methods in process engineering. In: Fun With Formal Methods, pp. 1–11 (2014)
4. Beillahi, S.M., Siddique, U., Tahar, S.: Formal analysis of power electronic systems. In: Butler, M., Conchon, S., Zaïdi, F. (eds.) ICFEM 2015. LNCS, vol. 9407, pp. 270–286. Springer, Cham (2015). doi:10.1007/978-3-319-25423-4_17
5. Binh, L.N.: Photonic Signal Processing: Techniques and Applications. Optical Science and Engineering. Taylor & Francis, London (2010)
6. Boca, P.P., Bowen, J.P., Siddiqi, J.I.: Formal Methods: State of the Art and New. Springer, London (2009)
7. Çapar, Ç., Goeckel, D., Paterson, K.G., Quaglia, E.A., Towsley, D., Zafer, M.: Signal-flow-based analysis of wireless security protocols. Inf. Comput. **226**, 37–56 (2013)
8. Dehghan, S.M., Mohamadian, M., Yazdian, A.: Hybrid electric vehicle based on bidirectional Z-source nine-switch inverter. IEEE Trans. Veh. Technol. **59**(6), 2641–2653 (2010)
9. Signal Flow Graph Similification Program for MATLAB (2014). http://www.mathworks.com/matlabcentral/fileexchange/22-mason-m
10. Gajanayake, C.J., Vilathgamuwa, D.M., Loh, P.C.: Small-signal and signal-flow-graph modeling of switched Z-source impedance network. IEEE Power Electron. Lett. **3**(3), 111–116 (2005)
11. Harrison, J.: Handbook of Practical Logic and Automated Reasoning. Cambridge University Press, New York (2009)
12. Hote, Y.V., Choudhury, D.R., Gupta, J.R.P.: Robust stability analysis of the PWM push-pull DC-DC converter. IEEE Trans. Power Electron. **24**(10), 2353–2356 (2009)
13. Isaksson, O., Keski-Seppala, S., Eppinger, S.D.: Evaluation of design process alternatives using signal flow graphs. In: ASME Design Engineering Technical Conferences, vol. 11(3), pp. 211–224 (2000)
14. Jennen, R., Max, S., Walke, B.: Frame delay distribution analysis of IEEE 802.11 networks using signal flow graphs. In: IEEE International Symposium on Personal, Indoor and Mobile Radio Communications, pp. 2035–2040 (2010)
15. Mason, S.J.: Feedback theory, further properties of signal flow graphs. In: Proceeding of Institute of Radio Engineers, vol. 44, pp. 920–926 (1956)
16. Mason, S.J.: Feedback theory, some properties of signal flow graphs. In: Proceeding of Institute of Radio Engineers, vol. 41, pp. 1144–1156 (1953)
17. Mason, S.J., Zimmermann, H.J.: Electronic Circuits, Signals, and Systems. Wiley, New York (1960)
18. Peng, F.Z.: Z-Source inverter. In: IAS Annual Meeting. Conference Record of the Industry Applications Conference, vol. 2, pp. 775–781 (2002)
19. Rajakaruna, S., Jayawickrama, Y.R.L.: Designing impedance network of Z-source inverters. In: International Power Engineering Conference, vol. 2, pp. 962–967 (2005)
20. Schmid, H.: Circuit transposition using signal-flow graphs. In: IEEE International Symposium on Circuits and Systems, vol. 2, pp. II-25–II-28 (2002)

21. Siddique, U., Beillahi, S.M., Tahar, S.: On the formal analysis of photonic signal processing systems. In: Núñez, M., Güdemann, M. (eds.) FMICS 2015. LNCS, vol. 9128, pp. 162–177. Springer, Cham (2015). doi:10.1007/978-3-319-19458-5_11
22. Sirawattananon, C., Bahadoran, M., Ali, J., Mitatha, S., Yupapin, P.P.: Analytical vernier effects of a PANDA ring resonator for microforce sensing application. IEEE Trans. Nanotechnol. **11**(4), 707–712 (2012)
23. Tarjan, R.: Depth first search and linear graph algorithms. SIAM J. Comput. **1**(2), 146–160 (1972)
24. Tiernan, J.C.: An efficient search algorithm to find the elementary circuits of a graph. Commun. ACM **13**(12), 722–726 (1970)

Computing a Correct and Tight Rounding Error Bound Using Rounding-to-Nearest

Sylvie Boldo[1,2]([✉])

[1] Inria, Université Paris-Saclay, 91893 Palaiseau, France
sylvie.boldo@inria.fr
[2] LRI, CNRS & Univ. Paris-Sud, 91405 Orsay, France

Abstract. When a floating-point computation is done, it is most of the time incorrect. The rounding error can be bounded by folklore formulas, such as $\varepsilon|x|$ or $\varepsilon|\circ(x)|$. This gets more complicated when underflow is taken into account as an absolute term must be considered. Now, let us compute this error bound in practice. A common method is to use a directed rounding in order to be sure to get an over-approximation of this error bound. This article describes an algorithm that computes a correct bound using only rounding to nearest, therefore without requiring a costly change of the rounding mode. This is formally proved using the Coq formal proof assistant to increase the trust in this algorithm.

1 Introduction

Floating-point (FP) arithmetic is the way computers deal with computations on real numbers. It is clearly defined [5,6], but it is not perfect. In particular, FP numbers have a finite precision, therefore even a single computation may be incorrect when the result does not fit in a FP number. This error is called a rounding error, and a part of the computer arithmetic literature tries to improve or bound these errors on some given algorithms.

The most common model for bounding this rounding error is the standard model [4] where

$$\circ(x) = x(1 + \delta) \qquad \text{with } |\delta| \leq u$$

with $\circ$ being the rounding to nearest and u being the machine epsilon, therefore 2^{-p} when p is the number of bits of the FP mantissa.

This model has two main drawbacks. The first one is that it does not take underflow into account. For example in `binary64`, if you round 3×2^{-1075}, you get the FP number 2×2^{-1074}, which gives a huge relative error of 33% compared to the input, but a small absolute error.

The second drawback is when this error bound needs to be computed. That is the case for example when considering midpoint-radius interval arithmetic [7]. Indeed, computing $\circ(2^{-p} \times \circ(x))$ may not be an overestimation of the error

---

S. Boldo—This work was supported by the FastRelax (ANR-14-CE25-0018-01) project of the French National Agency for Research (ANR).

S. Bogomolov et al. (Eds.): NSV 2016, LNCS 10152, pp. 47–51, 2017.
DOI: 10.1007/978-3-319-54292-8_4

bound. For example, let us consider $x = \frac{2^{-1022}+2^{-1074}}{2}$. Then $\circ(x) = 2^{-1023}$ and the error is 2^{-1075}. But $\circ\left(2^{-p} \times \circ(x)\right) = \circ\left(2^{-53} \times 2^{-1023}\right) = \circ\left(2^{-1076}\right) = 0$, which is *not* an overestimation of 2^{-1075}.

This article aims at providing a correct algorithm that computes a bound on the error of a FP operation. As we also want this algorithm to be fast, we wish to avoid changing the rounding mode, as it breaks the pipeline. We will therefore only consider rounding to nearest, both for the operation considered, and for our algorithm. Moreover, we want to prevent tests as they also break the pipeline.

More than a pen-and-paper proof, this work gives a high guarantee of its correctness and gives precise hypotheses on the needed precision and underflow threshold. We will rely on the Coq proof assistant. From the formal methods point of view, we will base our proof on the Flocq library [2]. Flocq is a formalization in Coq that offers a multi-radix and multi-precision formalization for various floating- and fixed-point formats (including FP with or without gradual underflow) with a comprehensive library of theorems. Its usability and practicality have been established against test-cases [1]. The corresponding Coq file is named **Error_bound_fp.v** and is available in the **example** directory of Flocq[1], available in the current git version, and in the next released versions $>2.5.1$.

Notations. We denote by $\circ$ the rounding to nearest, ties to even in radix 2. We denote by $\circ[\text{expr}]$ the rounding of the expression into brackets, where all the operations are considered to be rounded operations. For example, $\circ[3 \times x + y]$ denotes $\circ(\circ(3 \times x) + y)$. The smallest subnormal number is denoted by 2^{E_i} and the number of bits of the mantissa is $p > 0$. For basic knowledge about FP arithmetic (roundings, subnormal, error bounds), we refer the reader to [3,6].

2 Theorem

Theorem 1. *Let x be a real number. Assume that $E_i \leq -p$. Then*

$$|\circ(x) - x| \leq \circ\left[2^{-p} \times |\circ(x)| + 2^{E_i}\right].$$

The assumption is very light: $E_i \leq -p$ only means that 2^{-p} is in the format. It holds in all IEEE formats: for example in **binary64**, $p = 53$ and $E_i = -1074$ and in **binary32**, $p = 24$ and $E_i = -149$.

Proof. The first step is to prove that 2^{-p} and 2^{E_i} are in the format, therefore not rounded. This is trivial as long as $E_i \leq -p$.

Then, the error bound we are used to is $|\circ(x) - x| \leq 2^{-p} \times |\circ(x)| + 2^{E_i-1}$ or $\max\left(2^{-p} \times |\circ(x)|, 2^{E_i-1}\right)$. The first formula looks like our theorem, rounding excepted. The other difference is the 2^{E_i} instead of 2^{E_i-1}. Let us prove that the roundings do not endanger the result.

Let $t = \circ\left[2^{-p} \times |\circ(x)| + 2^{E_i}\right]$. Then, we split the proof into 4 cases, depending on the value of $|x|$.

---

[1] http://flocq.gforge.inria.fr/.

1. Assume $x = 0$. Then $\circ(x) = 0$, and $|\circ(x) - x| = 0$, while $t = \circ\left(0 + 2^{E_i}\right) = 2^{E_i}$. So the result holds.

2. Assume $0 < |x| < 2^{E_i+p}$. Then x has exponent E_i and $|\circ(x) - x| \leq \frac{1}{2}\mathrm{ulp}(x) = 2^{E_i-1}$. Moreover, $t = \circ\left[2^{-p} \times |\circ(x)| + 2^{E_i}\right] \geq \circ\left(2^{E_i}\right) = 2^{E_i}$. So the result holds.

3. Assume $2^{E_i+2p-1} \leq |x|$. Then $2^{-p} \times |\circ(x)| \geq 2^{E_i+p-1}$ and is normal. Therefore, the multiplication by 2^{-p} is correct and does not create any rounding error. Then $|\circ(x) - x| \leq 2^{-p} \times |\circ(x)| = \circ[2^{-p} \times |\circ(x)|] \leq \circ\left[2^{-p} \times |\circ(x)| + 2^{E_i}\right]$ by monotony of the rounding.

4. Assume $2^{E_i+p} \leq |x| < 2^{E_i+2p-1}$. This is the most complex case, as all roundings may go wrong. First $|\circ(x) - x| \leq 2^{-p} \times |\circ(x)|$. Let y be $2^{-p} \times |\circ(x)|$. Then $y < 2^{E_i+p-1}$ and is therefore in the subnormal range. As $|\circ(x) - x| \leq y$, what is left to prove is that $y \leq \circ\left(\circ(y) + 2^{E_i}\right)$. As y is small, $\circ(y)$ is a positive FP number in the subnormal range, therefore $\circ(y) + 2^{E_i}$ is also in the FP format and $\circ\left(\circ(y) + 2^{E_i}\right) = \circ(y) + 2^{E_i}$. What is left to prove is then $y \leq \circ(y) + 2^{E_i}$. Finally, as y is in the subnormal range, $|\circ(y) - y| \leq 2^{E_i-1}$. So $y \leq \circ(y) + 2^{E_i-1}$ and the result holds. $\square$

This pen-and-paper proof exactly corresponds to the Coq proof (as it was written from it). The itemized cases corresponding to the interval values of x become several lemmas in the Coq proof for the sake of readability.

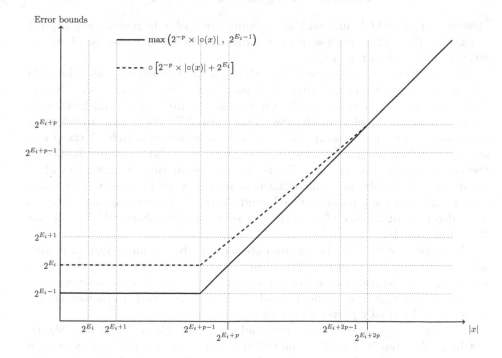

Fig. 1. Drawings comparing the error bounds of $\circ(x)$

3   Tightness of the Bound

The next question is how tight is the proved bound. In particular, is it much coarser than the usual bound? The answer is no and a graphical explanation is given in Fig. 1.

When $|x|$ is small, then the optimal bound is 2^{E_i-1}. As this bound is not a FP number, our algorithm returns the best possible bound, that is to say 2^{E_i}. When $|x|$ is big enough, meaning greater than 2^{E_i+2p} (that is 2^{-968} in binary64), we have the optimal bound, meaning $2^{-p} \times |\circ(x)|$. In this case, the 2^{E_i} is indeed negligible and is neglected as we use rounding to nearest (and not rounding towards $+\infty$). In the middle, meaning between 2^{E_i+p-1} and 2^{E_i+2p}, we have a slight overestimation compared to the usual bound. Note that this overestimation is bounded by 2^{E_i}.

4   Conclusion

We have formally proven that the following algorithm using only the rounding-to nearest mode:

$$\texttt{fabs(x)*0x1.p-53+0x1.p-1074}$$

gives a correct tight bound on the rounding error of x in rounding-to-nearest binary64. Note that overflow cannot happen here as all values involved are strictly smaller than the input x.

As for efficiency, random tests have shown it is quite efficient, as it involves neither tests, nor rounding change (2 flops plus the memory accesses). Nevertheless, on some architectures, subnormal numbers are trapped and handled in software, and are therefore much slower than normal FP operations. In this case, computing `x*0x1.p-53+0x1.p-1022` might be a better idea. Indeed, the previous theorem implies that $\circ\left[2^{-p} \times |\circ(x)| + 2^{E_i+p-1}\right]$ is also an overestimation of the rounding error. And as 2^{E_i+p-1} is the smallest normal number, this algorithm does not involve any subnormal number if x is not one and will be faster in most cases, at the price of a worse bound. A use of the processor max function may also prevent the use of operation on subnormal numbers, which is known to be quite costly.

A perspective is to be able to compute an error bound on a given rounding, using only this given rounding. The formula will probably need to be modified, for example suppressing the addition when rounding towards $+\infty$, negating twice the values when using rounding towards $-\infty$. But this needs to be worked out in depth and formally proved to get correct algorithms.

A harder perspective is to deal with radix 10. Then the multiplication should not be by 2^{-p}, but by 5×10^{-p}, and this multiplication is not always exact with big numbers, as was the case here with radix 2. The provided algorithm does therefore not hold in radix 10.

References

1. Boldo, S.: Deductive formal verification: how to make your floating-point programs behave. Thèse d'habilitation, Université Paris-Sud, October 2014
2. Boldo, S., Melquiond, G.: Flocq: a unified library for proving floating-point algorithms in Coq. In: Antelo, E., Hough, D., Ienne, P. (eds.) 20th IEEE Symposium on Computer Arithmetic, Tübingen, Germany, pp. 243–252 (2011)
3. Goldberg, D.: What every computer scientist should know about floating-point arithmetic. ACM Comput. Surv. **23**(1), 5–48 (1991)
4. Higham, N.J.: Accuracy and Stability of Numerical Algorithms, 2nd edn. SIAM (2002)
5. Microprocessor Standards Committee: IEEE Standard for Floating-Point Arithmetic. IEEE Std. 754-2008, pp. 1–58, August 2008
6. Muller, J.-M., Brisebarre, N., de Dinechin, F., Jeannerod, C.-P., Lefèvre, V., Melquiond, G., Revol, N., Stehlé, D., Torres, S.: Handbook of Floating-Point Arithmetic. Birkhäuser, Boston (2010)
7. Rump, S.M.: Fast and parallel interval arithmetic. BIT Numer. Math. **39**(3), 534–554 (1999)

Studying Sequences of Jumps in Hybrid Systems to Detect Zeno Phenomenon

Alexandre Chapoutot[(✉)] and Julien Alexandre dit Sandretto

U2IS, ENSTA ParisTech, Université Paris-Saclay,
828 bd des Maréchaux, 91762 Palaiseau Cedex, France
{alexandre.chapoutot,julien.alexandre-dit-sandretto}@ensta-paristech.fr

Abstract. We propose a numerical analysis of sequences of points of interest associated to the dynamics of hybrid systems. These sequences are made of instants of switching mode or instants when a particular quantity vanishes. This analysis allows one to discover instant of accumulation points, a.k.a. Zeno phenomenon. Some examples are given to show the potential of this approach.

Keywords: Numerical simulation · Hybrid automaton · Sequence transformations

1   Introduction

The behavior of hybrid systems, *i.e.*, their temporal evolution can be complex to analyze due to the mixing of discrete-time and continuous-time dynamics. Moreover, they can exhibit some behaviors, which are hard to predict such as Zeno phenomenon. In particular, Zeno behavior is difficult to infer automatically.

A usual way to study hybrid systems is based on numerical simulation for which several methods exist. Despite this approach suffers from numerical approximation, it also provides a view of the complexity of the dynamics. We propose in this article to use the results of numerical simulations to detect Zeno phenomenon in hybrid systems modeled by hybrid automata [9]. The main idea is to study particular sequences of values, for example, related to instants of mode switching.

From a numerical analysis point of view, simulating discrete dynamics (or jumps) involves detecting events usually through zero-crossing detection. A comprehensive survey of zero-crossing detection is given in [13]. The problem of Zeno phenomenon has been studied in many fields, a comprehensive overview is given in [10] in the context of set-based simulation. In [10] the handling of Zeno phenomenon is ensured by adding some constraints to hybrid automata such as energy functions. Our approach offers an alternative to the addition of constraints by trying to compute the time of accumulation point only by observing particular values of the dynamics.

This research was partially supported by the ANR INS Project CAFEIN (ANR-12-INSE-0007).

S. Bogomolov et al. (Eds.): NSV 2016, LNCS 10152, pp. 52–62, 2017.
DOI: 10.1007/978-3-319-54292-8_5

The article is organized as follows. In Sect. 2, we briefly recall the model of hybrid automata and how they are numerically simulated. We introduce the main mathematical tool used in this work, *i.e.*, *sequence transformations*, in Sect. 3. We provide some examples in Sect. 4 showing the effectiveness of our approach. Finally, we conclude and provide possible future work in Sect. 5.

2 Numerical Simulation of Hybrid Systems

2.1 Hybrid Automata

In this article, in order to facilitate the understanding of our method, we consider hybrid systems described by hybrid automata (HA).

We denote by $\mathbb{R}$ the set of real numbers, and by $\mathbb{B}$ the set of Boolean (containing two elements, $\top$ meaning true and $\bot$ meaning false). Given a function $x : \mathbb{R} \to \mathbb{R}^n$, we denote by $x^-(t)$ its left-limit.

Definition 1 (Hybrid automaton, [9]). *An n-dimensional hybrid automaton $\mathcal{H} = (L, F, E, G, R)$ is a tuple such that L is a finite set of locations, the function $F : L \to (\mathbb{R} \times \mathbb{R}^n \to \mathbb{R}^n)$ associates a flow equation to each location, $E \subseteq L \times L$ is a finite set of edges, $G : E \to (\mathbb{R}^n \to \mathbb{B})$ maps edges to guards and $R : E \to (\mathbb{R} \times \mathbb{R}^n \to \mathbb{R}^n)$ maps edges to reset maps.*

Notice that to simplify the presentation of our approach, we consider HA without invariant in each location. In other terms there is no constraint on the state variables. Besides, we assume that a transition $e = (\ell, \ell')$ is taken *as soon as $G(e)$ is true.*

Example 1. We consider the classical bouncing-ball system. So, the dynamics of the height y of the ball is given by

$$\dot{y}(t) = v_y(t), \qquad \dot{v}_y(t) = -g \qquad (1)$$

with the gravity constant on Earth $g = 9.8$. The HA has only one Location ℓ such that $F(\ell)$ is the flow defined by Eq. (1). There is also one edge $e = (\ell, \ell)$ representing the instant when the ball bounces on the floor, with a guard $G(e) := y \mapsto y \leqslant 0$ and a reset $R(e) = (t, (y, v_y)) \mapsto (y, -0.8v_y)$. ∎

The operational semantics of an HA [9] is a transition system with two kinds of transitions for the time elapse and the discrete jumps. From this operational semantics, we can define the trajectory of the HA, as in [7].

Definition 2 (Trajectory of an hybrid automaton). *Suppose given an HA $\mathcal{H} = (L, F, E, G, R)$. A state of $\mathcal{H}$ is a pair (x, ℓ) with $x \in \mathbb{R}^n$ and $\ell \in L$. A trajectory of $\mathcal{H}$, on the time interval $[t_0, t_f]$, starting from an initial state (x_0, ℓ_0), is a pair of functions $(x(t), \ell(t))$ with $x : [t_0, t_f] \to \mathbb{R}^n$ and $\ell : [t_0, t_f] \to L$, such that there exists time instants $t_0 \leqslant t_1 \leqslant \ldots \leqslant t_N = t_f$ satisfying, for every index i,*

1. x is continuous and ℓ is constant for all $t \in [t_i, t_{i+1}[$,
2. $x(0) = x_0$, $\ell(0) = \ell_0$,
3. $\forall t \in [t_i, t_{i+1}[$, $\dot{x}(t) = F(\ell(t))(t, x(t))$,
4. $\forall t \in]t_i, t_{i+1}[$, $\forall e = (\ell(t), \ell') \in E$, $G(e)(x(t)) = \bot$,
5. $G(e)(x^-(t_i)) = \top$ with $e = (\ell^-(t_i), \ell(t_i))$ and $x(t_i) = R(e)(t_i, x^-(t_i))$.

In Definition 2, the equations constraint the function x so that it conforms to the flow and jump conditions of $\mathcal{H}$. Condition 2 ensures that x satisfies the initial conditions, Condition 3 specifies that the dynamics of $x(t)$ is the flow at location $\ell(t)$, conditions 4 and 5 ensure that the time instants t_i are the instants where jumping conditions occur and that x evolves as described by reset maps when the corresponding guard is satisfied. Notice that we do not discuss conditions ensuring existence and uniqueness of trajectories as this is beyond the scope of this paper [8], but implicitly suppose that these are granted.

2.2   Numerical Solver

Numerical simulation aims at producing discrete approximations of the trajectories of an hybrid system $\mathcal{H}$ on the time interval $[t_0, t_f]$. We described in details in [2] how the simulation engine of Simulink operates, and briefly adapt here this simulation engine to HA.

Suppose that $\mathcal{H}$ is an HA, (x_0, ℓ_0) an initial state, and $(x(t), \ell(t))$ a trajectory of $\mathcal{H}$ starting from (x_0, ℓ_0). A numerical simulation algorithm computes a sequence $(t_k, x_k, \ell_k)_{k \in [0, N]}$ of time instants, state variable values and locations such that $\forall k \in [0, N]$, $x_k \approx x(t_k)$. Most of the difficulty lies in approximating the discrete jumps (instants where a guard becomes true), which are called *zero-crossings* in the numerical simulation community. In order to compute (t_k, x_k, ℓ_k), the following simulation loop is used, where h_k is the simulation step-size, that can be dynamically adapted in order to maintain a required precision,

1: **repeat**
2:      $x_{k+1} \leftarrow$ SolveODE$(F(\ell(t_k)), x_k, h_k)$ ▷ Solver step 1
3:      $(x_{k+1}, \ell_{k+1}) \leftarrow$ SolveZC(x_k, x_{k+1}) ▷ Solver step 2
4:      compute h_{k+1}
5:      $k \leftarrow k + 1$
6: **until** $t_k \geq t_f$

In the simulation loop, the solver first makes a continuous transition between instants t_k and $t_k + h_k$ under the assumption that no jump occurs (Solver step 1), and then it verifies this assumption (Solver step 2). If it turns out that there was a jump between t_k and $t_k + h_k$, the solver approximates as precisely as possible the time $t \in [t_k, t_k + h_k]$ at which this jump occurred. We briefly detail these both steps in the rest of this section.

Solver step 1. The continuous evolution of x between t_k and $t_k + h_k$ is described by $\dot{x}(t) = F(\ell(t_k))(t, x(t))$ and with initial condition $x(t_k) = x_k$. So, numerical simulation methods compute an approximation of the solution x at time $t_k + h_k$ of the initial value problem (IVP), with $f = F(\ell(t_k))$ such that

$$\dot{x}(t) = f(t, x(t)) \quad \text{and} \quad x(t_k) = x_k. \tag{2}$$

Note that we assume classical hypotheses on f ensuring existence and uniqueness of a solution of IVP, see [8] for more details. Usually, precise simulation algorithms often rely on a variable step solver, for which $(h_k)_{k\in\mathbb{N}}$ is not constant. The simplest is probably the Bogacki-Shampine method [12], also named ODE23. It computes x_{k+1} by

$$k_1 = f(t_k, x_k) \qquad k_2 = f(t_k + \frac{h_k}{2}, x_k + \frac{h_k}{2}k_1) \qquad k_3 = f(t_k + \frac{3h_k}{4}, x_k + \frac{3h_k}{4}k_2)$$
$$\tag{3a}$$

$$x_{k+1} = x_k + \frac{h_k}{9}(2k_1 + 3k_2 + 4k_3) \tag{3b}$$

$$k_4 = f(t_k + h_k, x_{k+1}) \qquad\qquad z_{k+1} = x_k + \frac{h_k}{24}(7k_1 + 6k_2 + 8k_3 + 3k_4) \tag{3c}$$

The value z_{k+1} defined in (3c) is a third order approximation of $x(t_k + h_k)$, whereas x_{k+1} is a second order approximation of this value, and is used to estimate the error $\text{Err} = |x_{k+1} - z_{k+1}|$. This error is compared to a given *tolerance* Tol and the step-size is changed accordingly: if the error is smaller then the step-size is *validated* and the step-size increased in order to speed up computations (in ODE23, next step-size is computed with $h_{k+1} = h_k \sqrt[3]{\text{Tol}/\text{Err}}$), if the error Err is greater then the step-size is *rejected* and the computation is tried again with the smaller step-size $h_k/2$. We refer to [8, p. 167] for a complete description on such numerical methods.

Solver step 2. Once x_k and x_{k+1} computed, the solver checks if there were a jump in the time interval $[t_k, t_{k+1}]$. In order to do so, it tests for each edge e starting from ℓ_k whether $G(e)(x_k)$ is false and $G(e)(x_{k+1})$ is true. If there is no such edge, then it is considered that no jump occurred, we set $\ell_{k+1} = \ell_k$ and continue the simulation. Notice this technique does not guarantee the detection of all events occurring between $[t_k, t_{k+1}]$ as explained in [13] or [6].

   If the solver finds such an edge, this means that there was a jump on $[t_k, t_{k+1}]$ and we must approximate the first time instant $\xi \in [t_k, t_k + h_k]$ such that $G(e)(x(\xi))$ is true. To do so, the solver encloses ξ in an interval $[t_l, t_r]$ starting with $t_l = t_k$ and $t_r = t_k + h_k$, and reduces this interval until the time precision $|t_l - t_r|$ is smaller than a given threshold. To reduce the width of the interval, the solver first makes a guess for ξ using a linear extrapolation and then computes an approximation of $x(\xi)$ using a polynomial interpolation of x on $[t_k, t_k + h_k]$. Depending on $G(e)(x(\xi))$, it then sets $t_l = \xi$ or $t_r = \xi$ and starts over. In the case of Hermite interpolation (which is the method used together with the ODE23 solver), the polynomial interpolation is given, for $t \in [t_k, t_k + h_k]$, by

$$x(t) \approx (2\tau^3 - 3\tau^2 + 1)x_k + (\tau^3 - 2\tau^2 + \tau)h_k\dot{x}_k + (-2\tau^3 + 3\tau^2)x_{k+1} + (\tau^3 - \tau^2)h_k\dot{x}_{k+1}$$
$$\tag{4}$$

where $\tau = (t - t_k)/h_k$, and $\dot{x}_k$, $\dot{x}_{k+1}$ are approximations of the derivative of x at t_k, t_{k+1} given by $F(x(t_k))$ and $F(x(t_{k+1}))$ respectively. For more details on zero-crossing algorithms, we refer to [2,13].

From the results of Solver step 2, we can generate sequences of values, for example, instants of mode switching. In particular, if these sequences of values converge to a finite limit this may exhibit a Zeno phenomenon. To study these sequences of values, we use *sequence transformations* methods.

3   Acceleration of Sequence Convergence

Convergence acceleration techniques, also named *sequence transformations*, allow one to increase the rate of convergence of a sequence. In numerical analysis, there are several convergence acceleration methods, they transform convergent sequences (which approach their limits slowly) into sequences which converge more quickly to the same limit.

3.1   General Definitions

Before giving an overview of sequence transformation techniques (for more details, we refer to [4]), we recall some basic definitions of *metric spaces* and *sequence convergence* [11].

Definition 3 (Metric space). *A metric space is a pair $\langle D, d \rangle$ where D is a non-empty set and d is a metric on D, i.e., a function $d : D \times D \to \mathbb{R}^+$, such that $\forall x, y \in D$ we have*

- $d(x, y) = 0 \Leftrightarrow x = y$.
- $d(x, y) = d(y, x)$.
- $d(x, y) \leqslant d(x, z) + d(z, y), \forall z \in D$.

The set of sequences over D (denoted by $D^{\mathbb{N}}$) is the set of functions between $\mathbb{N}$ and D.

Definition 4 (Convergent sequence). *A sequence $(x_n) \in D^{\mathbb{N}}$ converges to $v \in D$ if and only if we have*

$$\lim_{n \to \infty} d(x_n, v) = 0 .$$

Definition 5 (Sequence transformation). *Let a sequence $(x_n) \in D^{\mathbb{N}}$ converge to $v \in D$. A sequence transformation is a function $T : D^{\mathbb{N}} \to D^{\mathbb{N}}$ (T denotes a particular acceleration method) such that: if $(y_n) = T(x_n)$ then (y_n) converges to v faster than (x_n), i.e.,*

$$\lim_{n \to \infty} \frac{d(y_n, v)}{d(x_n, v)} = 0 .$$

This means that (y_n) is asymptotically closer to v than (x_n).

As mentioned before, there are several sequence transformations changing convergent sequences into sequences which converge more quickly to the same limit. Nevertheless, each sequence transformation only increases the rate of convergence of some classes of sequences. These classes are related to the *kernel* of transformation methods, formally defined in Definition 6.

Definition 6 (Kernel of sequence transformations). *Let T be a sequence transformation. The kernel θ_T of T is the set of sequences $(x_n) \in D^{\mathbb{N}}$, for which T transforms (x_n) to the constant sequence $v \in D$. More precisely,*

$$\theta_T = \left\{ (x_n) \in D^{\mathbb{N}} : \exists v \in \mathbb{R}, \forall n \in \mathbb{N}, T(x_n) = v \right\}.$$

For the rest of this section, we present only sequence transformations for real sequences, the extension to sequences on any metric space D is straightforward. We now present one acceleration method that we used in our experiments described in Sect. 4.

The Aitken Method. It is probably the most famous sequence transformation. Given a sequence $(x_n) \in \mathbb{R}^{\mathbb{N}}$, the accelerated sequence (y_n) is defined by

$$\forall n \in \mathbb{N}, \ y_n = x_n - \frac{(x_{n+1} - x_n)^2}{x_{n+2} - 2x_{n+1} + x_n}. \tag{5}$$

It should be noted that in order to compute y_n for some $n \in \mathbb{N}$, three values of (x_n) are required: x_n, x_{n+1} and x_{n+2}.

Example 2. To illustrate Aitken method, we apply it to the following sequence

$$\forall n \in \mathbb{N}, \quad s_n = 1 + \frac{1}{n+1} \quad \text{with} \quad \lim_{n \to +\infty} s_n = 1.$$

The obtained results are given in Fig. 1. We can see that the value of the 7th element of the accelerated sequence is closer to the limit by a factor of two. ∎

The kernel K_{Aitken} of Aitken method is the set of all sequences of the form $x_n = s + a.\lambda^n$ where s, a and λ are real constants such that $a \neq 0$ and $\lambda \neq 1$ (see [5] for more details). Note that the Aitken method is an efficient method for accelerating sequences, but it highly suffers from numerical instabilities when x_n, x_{n+1} and x_{n+2} are close to each other.

4 Experiments

We report in this section, application of sequence transformation techniques to study Zeno phenomenon in hybrid systems. We consider classical examples such as the bouncing ball system and the two tanks system. Computations are done with Matlab2015a using numerical solver ODE23 and zero-crossing methods as explained in Sect. 2.2.

Rank	Initial sequence	Rank	Accelerated sequence
0	2.0		
1	1.5		
2	1.3333333	0	1.25
3	1.25	1	1.16666667
4	1.2	2	1.125
5	1.1666667	3	1.1
6	1.1428571	4	1.0833333
7	1.125	5	1.0714286
8	1.1111111	6	1.0625
9	1.1	7	1.0555556
⋮	⋮	⋮	⋮

Fig. 1. The results obtained with the Aitken method on the sequence $s_n = 1 + \dfrac{1}{n+1}$.

4.1 Bouncing Ball

Consider again Example 1 of the bouncing ball system. We will study the following sequences of values

1. the sequence of time instants, denoted by t_b, at which the ball hits the ground.
2. the sequence of time instants, denoted by t_v, at which the height goes from increasing to decreasing, *i.e.*, when the velocity becomes zero.
3. the sequence of values, denoted by v, of the height of the ball when the velocity is zero.

In Fig. 2, a trajectory with a numerical simulation is given. The red bullets represent the values of Sequence 1 and the Sequence 3. Clearly, we can observe that the two sequences converge towards a particular value in time and with a zero height.

For this particular example, we know that the sequence of time instances at which the ball bounces follow a geometric series which has for limit the value t^* such that

$$t^* = \frac{1}{g}\left(v_0 + v_1\left(\frac{1+\gamma}{1-\gamma}\right)\right) \quad \text{with} \quad v_1 = \sqrt{v_0^2 + 2gx_0} \ .$$

The values x_0 and v_0 are respectively the initial position and the initial velocity of the ball while γ stands for the coefficient of restitution of the ball. In Example 1, we have $\gamma = 0.8$, and we consider the initial values $x_0 = 0$ and $v_0 = 20$ so that $t^* = 40.774719673802245$.

From the numerical simulation, we obtained the following first values of t_b, t_v and v:

$$t_b = (4.0775, 7.7472, 11.0499, 14.0224, 16.6977, 19.1054, \dots)$$
$$t_v = (2.0387, 5.9123, 9.3986, 12.5362, 15.3600, 17.9015, \dots)$$
$$v = (20.3874, 16.5138, 13.3761, 10.8347, 8.7761, 7.1086, \dots)$$

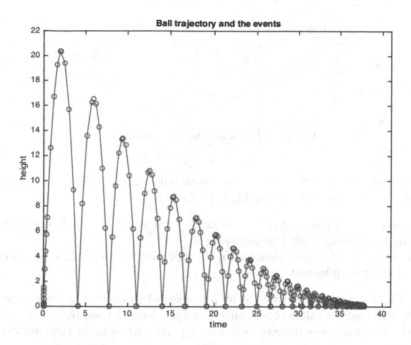

Fig. 2. Numerical simulation result for the bouncing-ball system

Applying the Aitken method on these sequences of values, we get

$$\text{Aitken}(t_b) = (0, 0, 40.7747, 40.7747, 40.7747, 40.7747, \dots)$$
$$\text{Aitken}(t_v) = (0, 0, 40.7747, 40.7747, 40.7747, 40.7747, \dots)$$
$$\text{Aitken}(v) = 10^{-10} \times (0, 0, 0.6171, -0.2908, 0.3606, -0.0039, \dots)$$

We observe that the accelerated sequences associated to t_b and t_v converges towards the limit 40.7747 which seems to be the accumulation point in time of the Zeno phenomenon. Moreover, the accelerated sequence associated to v converges very quickly to zero indicating that at the accumulation point the height of the ball is zero. Note that all the accelerated sequences start with two zero values due to the initialization of the algorithm, *i.e.*, Aitken method needs three values to produce an output.

This initialization phase may be a problem to study hybrid systems for which ones the amount of data available is not enough.

4.2 Two Tanks

We consider another classical example of hybrid systems exhibiting a Zeno phenomenon that is a two tanks system [10]. The hybrid automaton associated to the two tanks system is given in Fig. 3. Variable y_1 stands for the variation of water height in Tank 1 while y_2 is the variation of water height in Tank 2.

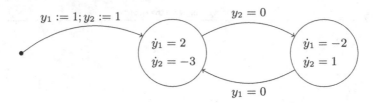

Fig. 3. Hybrid automaton of two tanks

We study the sequences of values associated to state variable y_1 (we could also apply the same idea on variable y_2) which are

1. the sequence of time instants, denoted by t, at which the mode is switching, going from filling Tank 1 to emptying it.
2. the sequence of values, denoted by h, standing for the height of water in Tank 1 for each instant in t.

In Fig. 4, a trajectory obtained by a numerical simulation is given. The red bullets represent the values of Sequence 1 and Sequence 2. Clearly, we can observe that the two sequences converge towards a particular value in time and to the value zero.

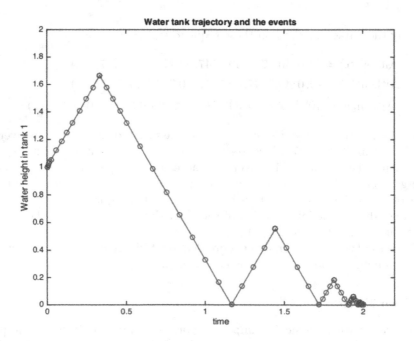

Fig. 4. Numerical simulation result of the two tanks system

From the numerical simulation, we have the following first values of t and h:

$$t = (0.3333, 1.4444, 1.8148, 1.9383, 1.9794, 1.9931, \dots)$$
$$h = (1.6667, 0.5556, 0.1852, 0.0617, 0.0206, 0.0069, \dots)$$

Applying the Aitken method on these sequences of values, we get

$$\text{Aitken}(t) = (0, 0, 2.0, 2.0, 2.0, 2.0, \dots)$$
$$\text{Aitken}(h) = 10^{-12} \times (0, 0, 0.1268, 0.0004, 0.0208, -0.0844, \dots)$$

We observe that the accelerated sequence associated to t converges towards the limit 2.0 which seems to be the accumulation point in time of the Zeno phenomenon. Moreover, the accelerated sequence associated to h converges very quickly to zero indicating that at the accumulation point the height of the water is zero.

5   Conclusion

We presented a new method to detect Zeno phenomenon in hybrid systems. This method only uses observation of points of interest in numerical simulation results. It does not modified the initial model with constraints such as in [10] to infer the time of accumulation.

The next work is to apply our method on more complex examples to prove its scalability and its robustness. The second next work is to adapt such techniques to the framework of set-based simulation [1,3,10] in order to have safe results. In particular, a simple approach would be to applied sequence transformation methods on the sequences of bounds of the intervals produced by set-based simulation.

References

1. Alexandre dit Sandretto, J., Chapoutot, A.: DynBEX: a differential constraint library for studying dynamical systems. In: Conference on Hybrid Systems: Computation and Control (HSCC 2016), Vienne, Austria, April 2016
2. Bouissou, O., Chapoutot, A.: An operational semantics for Simulink's simulation engine. In: Languages, Compliers, Tools, and Theory for Embedded Systems, pp. 129–138. ACM (2012)
3. Bouissou, O., Chapoutot, A., Mimram, S.: HySon: precise simulation of hybrid systems with imprecise inputs. In: Rapid System Prototyping. IEEE (2012)
4. Brezinski, C., Redivo Zaglia, M.: Extrapolation Methods-Theory and Practice. North-Holland, Amsterdam (1991)
5. Brezinski, C., Redivo Zaglia, M.: Generalizations of Aitken's process for accelerating the convergence of sequences. Comput. Appl. Math. 26(2), 171–189 (2007)
6. Esposito, J.M., Kumar, V., Pappas, G.J.: Accurate event detection for simulating hybrid systems. In: Benedetto, M.D., Sangiovanni-Vincentelli, A. (eds.) HSCC 2001. LNCS, vol. 2034, pp. 204–217. Springer, Heidelberg (2001). doi:10.1007/3-540-45351-2_19

7. Goebel, R., Hespanha, J., Teel, A.R., Cai, C., Sanfelice, R.: Hybrid systems: Generalized solutions and robust stability. In: IFAC NOLCOS, pp. 1–12 (2004)
8. Hairer, E., Nørsett, S.P., Wanner, G.: Solving Ordinary Differential Equations I: Nonstiff Problems. Springer, Heidelberg (1993)
9. Henzinger, T.A.: The theory of hybrid automata. In: Symposium on Logic in Computer Science, pp. 278–292. IEEE Computer Society Press (1996)
10. Konečný, M., Taha, W., Bartha, F.A., Duracz, J., Duracz, A., Ames, A.D.: Enclosing the behavior of a hybrid automaton up to and beyond a zeno point. Nonlinear Anal. Hybrid Syst. **20**, 1–20 (2016)
11. Rudin, W.: Principles of Mathematical Analysis. McGraw-Hill, New York (1976)
12. Shampine, L., Gladwell, I., Thompson, S.: Solving ODEs with MATLAB. Cambridge Univ. Press, Cambridge (2003)
13. Zhang, F., Yeddanapudi, M., Mosterman, P.J.: Zero-crossing location and detection algorithms for hybrid system simulation. In: IFAC World Congress, pp. 7967–7972 (2008)

Toward a Standard Benchmark Format
and Suite for Floating-Point Analysis

Nasrine Damouche[1]([⊠]), Matthieu Martel[1], Pavel Panchekha[2], Chen Qiu[2],
Alexander Sanchez-Stern[2], and Zachary Tatlock[2]

[1] Université de Perpignan Via Domitia, Perpignan, France
nasrine.damouche@univ-perp.fr
[2] University of Washington, Seattle, USA

Abstract. We introduce FPBench, a standard benchmark format for
validation and optimization of numerical accuracy in floating-point computations. FPBench is a first step toward addressing an increasing need in
our community for comparisons and combinations of tools from different
application domains. To this end, FPBench provides a basic floating-
point benchmark format and accuracy measures for comparing different
tools. The FPBench format and measures allow comparing and composing different floating-point tools. We describe the FPBench format and
measures and show that FPBench expresses benchmarks from recent
papers in the literature, by building an initial benchmark suite drawn
from these papers. We intend for FPBench to grow into a standard
benchmark suite for the members of the floating-point tools research
community.

1 Introduction

The increasingly urgent demand for reliable software has led to tremendous
advances in automatic program analysis and verification [4–6,8,18]. However,
these techniques have typically focused on integer programs, and do not apply to
the floating-point computations we depend on for safety-critical control in avionics or medical devices, nor the analyses carried out by scientific and computer-
aided design applications. In these contexts, floating-point accuracy is critical since subtle rounding errors can lead to significant discrepancies between
floating-point results and the real results developers expect. Indeed, floating-
point arithmetic is notoriously unintuitive and its sensitivity to roundoff errors
makes such computations fiendishly difficult to debug. Traditionally, such errors
have been addressed by numerical methods experts who manually analyze and
rewrite floating-point code to ensure accuracy and stability. However, these man-
ual techniques are difficult to apply and typically do not lead to independently
checkable certificates guaranteeing program accuracy.

The research community has responded to these challenges by developing
a rich array of automated techniques that provide guaranteed bounds on the
accuracy of floating-point computations or attempt to automatically improve

© Springer International Publishing AG 2017
S. Bogomolov et al. (Eds.): NSV 2016, LNCS 10152, pp. 63–77, 2017.
DOI: 10.1007/978-3-319-54292-8_6

accuracy. For example, Fluctuat [12,13], used in many companies, performs static analysis of C programs to prove a bound on the rounding errors introduced by the use of floating-point numbers instead of reals. Fluctuat also helps users debug floating-point errors by detecting the operations responsible for significant precision loss. Salsa [10] automatically improves the numerical accuracy of programs by using an abstract interpretation to guide transformations that minimize the errors arising during computations. Herbie [21] uses a heuristic search to improve the numerical accuracy of an arithmetic expression by estimating and localizing the roundoff errors of an expression using sampled points, applying a set of rules in order to improve the accuracy of the expression and combining these improvements for different input domains. Rosa [11] combines an exact SMT solver on reals with sound affine arithmetic to verify accuracy post-conditions from assertions about the accuracy of inputs. Rosa can guarantee that the desired precision can be soundly obtained in a finite-precision implementation when propagation error is included. Finally, FPTaylor [24] improves on interval arithmetic by using Taylor series to narrow the computed error bounds.

As the number of tools dedicated to analyzing and improving numerical accuracy grows, it becomes increasingly difficult to make fair comparisons between the techniques. This is because each tool is targeted to slightly different domains, uses slightly different formats for expressing benchmarks, and reports results using related but slightly different measures. Furthermore, without any standard set of floating-point benchmarks, it is difficult to identify opportunities for composing complementary tools.

To address these challenges, the floating-point research community needs a standard benchmark format and common set of measures that enables comparison and cooperation between tools. This goal is motivated by the success of standard benchmark suites like SPEC [17] and SPLASH-2 [25] in the compiler community, the DIMACS [1] format in the SAT-solving community, and the SMT-LIB [3] format in the SMT-solving community. The formats have enabled fair comparisons between tools, crisp characterizations of the tradeoffs between different approaches, and useful cooperation between tools with complementary strengths.

In this article, we propose FPBench, a general floating-point format and benchmark suite. FPBench describes a common format and a suite of accuracy measurements; we envision floating-point tools taking in FPBench formatted programs and using the FPBench accuracy measures to describe accuracy. This allows users to combine tools that perform complementary tasks and compare competing tools to choose the one best for their task. The common scientific methodology FPBench enables is crucial for demonstrating the improvements of each tool on the state of the art.

The main contributions of this article are the following:

(i) A uniform format for expressing floating-point benchmarks, FPCore.
(ii) A set of utilities for converting to and from FPCore programs, and working with FPCore programs.

(iii) A set of measures on which to evaluate various floating-point tools on FPBench benchmarks.

(iv) An initial suite of benchmarks drawing from existing floating-point literature.

The remainder of this article is organized as follows. Section 2, describes the FPBench formats. Section 3 describes the accuracy measures. Section 4 describes the utilities FPBench provides to support creating and working with benchmarks. Section 5 surveys our existing benchmark suite, highlighting representative case studies from recent tools in the literature. Finally, Sect. 6 discusses future work and concludes.

2   Benchmark Format

FPBench provides a common input format for floating-point tools. This format makes it possible to develop a collection of floating-point benchmarks common to our research community, and also allows users to compose floating-point tools. So, a common floating-point benchmark format must be easy to parse, have simple and clear semantics, support floating-point details, and be expressive enough for many domains. To satisfy these requirements, FPBench provides the FPCore format, a minimal expression-based language for floating-point computations. A common floating-point benchmark format must also be easy to translate to and from popular industrial languages like C, C++, Matlab, and Fortran. To satisfy these requirements, FPBench also provides the extended FPImp format, a basic imperative language for floating-point computations which can be automatically compiled to FPCore.

2.1   FPCore

FPCore is an S-expression format featuring mathematical functions, if statements, and while loops. All floating-point functions from C11's math.h and all Fortran 2003 intrinsics are supported operators, as well as standard arithmetic operators like addition and comparison; likewise, all constants defined in C11's math.h are available as constants. Following IEEE754 and common C and Fortran runtimes, FPCore does not prescribe the accuracy of built-in mathematical functions. However, individual benchmarks can declare the accuracy they assume for built-in operations which analyzers can take into account.

A FPCore benchmark specifies a set of inputs, a floating-point expression, and optional meta-data flags such as a name, citations, preconditions on inputs, and the floating-point precision (binary32, binary64, ...) used to evaluate that benchmark. The full FPCore syntax is as follows:[1]

---

[1] Not shown in the grammar: FPBench uses ";" to indicate that the remainder of a line is a comment.

$\langle FPCore \rangle ::= (\text{'FPCore'} (\langle identifier \rangle^*) \langle property \rangle^* \langle expression \rangle)$

$\langle expression \rangle ::= \langle constant \rangle \mid \langle identifier \rangle \mid (\langle operation \rangle \langle expression \rangle^*)$
$\quad \mid (\text{'if'} \langle expression \rangle \langle expression \rangle \langle expression \rangle)$
$\quad \mid (\text{'while'} \langle expression \rangle (\langle loopvar \rangle^*) \langle expression \rangle)$
$\quad \mid (\text{'let'} (\langle binding \rangle^*) \langle expression \rangle)$

$\langle loopvar \rangle ::= [\langle identifier \rangle \langle expression \rangle \langle expression \rangle]$

$\langle constant \rangle ::= \langle number \rangle \mid \text{'E'} \mid \text{'LOG2E'} \mid \text{'LOG10E'} \mid \text{'LN2'} \mid \text{'LN10'} \mid \text{'PI'} \mid \cdots$

$\langle operation \rangle ::= \text{'+'} \mid \text{'*'} \mid \text{'<'} \mid \cdots \mid \text{'abs'} \mid \text{'acos'} \mid \text{'and'} \mid \text{'asin'} \mid \cdots$

$\langle property \rangle ::= \langle propname \rangle \langle propval \rangle$

$\langle propname \rangle ::= \text{':name'} \mid \text{':cite'} \mid \text{':pre'} \mid \text{':type'} \mid \cdots$

$\langle propval \rangle ::= \langle expression \rangle \mid \langle string \rangle \mid (\langle identifier \rangle^*) \mid \langle identifier \rangle$

$\langle binding \rangle ::= [\langle identifier \rangle \langle expression \rangle]$

Since the language is S-expression based, parentheses and braces are literals. The semantics of these programs is ordinary function evaluation, with `let` bindings evaluated simultaneously and `while` loops evaluated by simultaneously updating the loop variables until the condition is true, and then evaluating the return value:

$$\frac{H : x_i^0 \Downarrow v_i \qquad H[x_i \mapsto v_i]_i : c \Downarrow \top}{H[x_i \mapsto v_i]_i : e_i \Downarrow x_i' \qquad H : (\text{while } c \ ([x_i \ x_i' \ e_i]_i) \ y) \Downarrow v}{H : (\text{while } c \ ([x_i \ x_i^0 \ e_i]_i) \ y) \Downarrow v}$$

$$\frac{H : x_i^0 \Downarrow v_i \qquad H[x_i \mapsto v_i]_i : c \Downarrow \bot \qquad H[x_i \mapsto v_i]_i : y \Downarrow v}{H : (\text{while } c \ ([x_i \ x_i^0 \ e_i]_i) \ y) \Downarrow v}$$

The optional properties are used to record additional information about each benchmark. Benchmarks are currently annotated with a `:name`, a `:description` of the benchmark and its inputs, the floating-point `:type` (either `binary32` or `binary64`), a precondition `:pre`, and a citation `:cite`. All FPBench tools ignore unknown attributes, so they represent an easy way to record additional benchmark information. We recommend that properties specific to a single tool be prefixed with the name of the tool.

2.2 FPImp

Where FPCore is the format consumed by tools, FPImp is a format for simplifying the translation from imperative languages to FPCore. While FPCore is a functional language with a minimal set of features for representing floating-point computations, FPImp includes common imperative features like variable assignments, multiple return values, and multi-way `if` statements. More complex features, such as arrays, pointers, records, and recursive function calls, are left to future language extensions. In our experience, translating C, Fortran, and Matlab to FPImp is relatively easy. FPImp has expressions similar to those in FPCore, but without if, while, and let expressions; these are instead replaced with statements. The FPImp syntax is as follows:

⟨*FPImp*⟩ ::= ('FPImp' (⟨*identifier*⟩*) ⟨*property*⟩* ⟨*statement*⟩* ⟨*output*⟩)

⟨*output*⟩ ::= ('output' ⟨*expression*⟩*)

⟨*expression*⟩ ::= ⟨*constant*⟩ | ⟨*identifier*⟩ | (⟨*operation*⟩ ⟨*expression*⟩*)

⟨*statement*⟩ ::= ['=' ⟨*identifier*⟩ ⟨*expression*⟩]
    | ('if' ⟨*ifbranch*⟩*)
    | ('while' ⟨*expression*⟩ ⟨*statement*⟩*)

⟨*ifbranch*⟩ ::= [⟨*expression*⟩ ⟨*statement*⟩*]
    | ['else' ⟨*statement*⟩*]

As in FPCore, each FPImp benchmark includes free parameters and properties; as an imperative language, it includes a list of program statements and multiple return values instead of a single body expression. Assignments and while loops behave in the usual way. Expressions in FPImp are evaluated similarly to FPCore expressions. An if statement defines a many-way branch; any else branch must be the last branch in its if. The output statement can return several values and appears at the end of a function.

The FPImp to FPCore compiler translates FPImp functions to FPCore benchmarks while retaining all properties and keeping the same set of free parameters. It inlines assignments, converts the imperative bodies of FPImp loops to the simultaneous-assignment loops of FPCore, replaces many-way if statements with nested if s, and generates multiple FPCore benchmarks for FPImp programs with multiple outputs.

3   Accuracy Measurements

To compare floating-point tools, a common input format is not enough: a common measure of accuracy is also necessary. FPBench thus defines a collection of accuracy measures to allow tools to rigorously describe the accuracy measure they use. Given the diversity of accuracy measures in the literature, standardizing on a single accuracy measure would be difficult, and could harm the development of some classes of tools. Instead, FPBench standardizes several measures of accuracy; tools that measure accuracy should state which of the FPBench accuracy measures they use to compare tools.

3.1   Measurement Axes

Floating-point accuracy is best analyzed along several axes: scaling vs non-scaling error, forward vs. backward error, maximum vs. average error. Tools that measure error may use sound vs. statistical techniques, and tools that transform programs have several options for how to measure accuracy improvement.

Scaling vs non-scaling error (ε). There are several ways to measure the error of producing the inaccurate value $\hat{x}$ instead of the true value x. Two common mathematical notions are the absolute and relative error:

$$\varepsilon_{\text{abs}}(x, x') = |x - \hat{x}| \quad \text{and} \quad \varepsilon_{\text{rel}}(x, x') = \left| \frac{x - \hat{x}}{x} \right|$$

Relative error scales with the quantity being measured, and thus makes sense for measuring both large and small numbers, much like the floating-point format itself. A notion of error more closely tied to the floating-point format is the Units in the Last Place (ULPs)[2] difference. Some tools instead use the logarithm of the ULPs, which approximately describes the number of incorrect low-order bits in $\hat{x}$. These two measures are defined as:[3]

$$\varepsilon_{\text{ulps}}(x, x') = |\mathbb{F} \cap [\min(x, \hat{x}), \max(x, \hat{x})]| \quad \text{and} \quad \varepsilon_{\text{bits}}(x, x') = \log_2 \varepsilon_{\text{ulps}}(x, x')$$

The floating-point numbers are distributed roughly exponentially, so this measure of error scales in a similar manner to relative error; however, it is better-behaved in the presence of denormal numbers and infinities.

Forward vs. backward error (ε). Forward error and backward error are two common measures for the error of a mathematical *computation*. For a true function f and its approximation $\hat{f}$, forward error measures the difference between outputs for a fixed input, while backward error measures the difference between inputs for a fixed output. Formally,[4]

$$\epsilon_{fwd}(f, \hat{f}, x) = \varepsilon(f(x), \hat{f}(x))$$

$$\epsilon_{bwd}(f, \hat{f}, x) = \min \left\{ \varepsilon(x, x') : x' \in \mathbb{F}^n \wedge \hat{f}(x') = f(x) \right\}.$$

Backward error is important for evaluating the stability of an algorithm, and in scientific applications where multiple sources of error (algorithmic error vs. sensor error) must be compared. Existing tools typically measure forward error because backward error can be tricky to compute for floating-point computations, where there may not be an input that produces the true output.

Average vs. maximum error (E). Describing the error of a floating-point computation means summarizing its behavior across multiple inputs. Existing tools use either maximum or average error for this task. Formally,[5]

$$E_{\max}(f, \hat{f}) = \max \left\{ \epsilon(f, \hat{f}, x) : x \in \mathbb{F}^n \right\} \quad \text{and} \quad E_{\text{avg}}(f, \hat{f}) = \frac{1}{N} \sum_{x \in \mathbb{F}^n} \epsilon(f, \hat{f}, x).$$

---

[2] Unfortunately, this term means different things in the mathematical and programming communities. We use the definition common for programming tools [19, 21, 23].

[3] We are using $|S|$ to denote the number of elements in a set S.

[4] Where n is the number of arguments.

[5] Where N is the number of valid inputs, and n is the number of arguments.

Worst-case error tends to be easier to measure soundly, while average error tends to be easier to measure statistically.

Sound vs. statistical techniques. Running a floating-point program on all valid inputs is intractable. Existing tools either soundly overapproximate the error using static analysis or approximate the error using statistical sampling.

Most static techniques are based on interval or affine arithmetic to over-approximate floating-point arithmetic, often using abstract interpretation. Abstract interpretation may use either non-relational [20] or relational abstract domains [2,7,14], and may use acceleration techniques (widenings [9]) to over-approximate loops without unrolling them. While such techniques tend to provide loose over-approximations of the floating-point error of programs, they are fast and provide sound error bounds. In some embedded applications, correctness is critical and unsound techniques will not do.

In domains where correctness is not absolutely critical, sampling can provide tight approximations of error. Many sampling techniques are used, including naive random samples [21] and Markov-chain Monte Carlo [23]. These techniques involve running a program multiple times, so tend to be slower than static analysis.

Measuring improvement (ι). Tools that *transform* floating-point programs need to compare the accuracy of two floating-point programs: the original and the transformed. Several comparison measures are possible. Comparisons can use the improvement in worst-case or average error between the original $\hat{f}$ and improved $\hat{f}'$ implementation of the same mathematical function f:

$$\iota_{\mathrm{imp}} = E(f, \hat{f}) - E(f, \hat{f}')$$

However, one cannot usually improve the accuracy of a computation simultaneously on all inputs. It is thus often necessary to make a computation less accurate on some points to make it more accurate overall. In this case, it may be useful to report the largest unimprovement, which measures the cost of improving accuracy:

$$\iota_{\mathrm{wrs}}(\hat{f}, \hat{f}') = \max \left\{ \epsilon(f, \hat{f}', x) - \epsilon(f, \hat{f}', x) \; : \; x \in \mathbb{F}^n \right\}$$

Other measures, such as those describing the trade-off between accuracy and speed, are also interesting, but are less commonly used in the literature and thus not standardized in FPBench. Improvement tools could also estimate their effect on numerical stability using automatic differentiation [15] or Lyapunov exponents [22], but we do not know of any such tools.

3.2   Existing Tools

The error measures described can be applied to categorize the error measurements used by existing tools. Table 1 compares Fluctuat [12], FPTaylor [24], Herbie [21], Rosa [11], and Salsa [10].

Table 1. A comparison of how five floating-point measure error across the axes identified in this section.

Fluctuat	Absolute	Forward	Max	Sound	
FPTaylor	Absolute	Forward	Max	Sound	
Herbie	Bits	Forward	Average	Statistical	Improvement
Rosa	Absolute	Forward	Max	Sound	
Salsa	Absolute	Forward	Max	Sound	Improvement
STOKE	ULPs	Forward	Max	Statistical	Improvement

Fluctuat, FPTaylor, and Rosa all verify error bounds on the accuracy of floating-point computations. Given their need for soundness, it is natural that they use sound error analyses and estimate maximum error. Their use of absolute forward error derives from the difficulty of approximating the other forms of error statically. Herbie and Salsa are tools for improving the accuracy of programs, but differ dramatically in their approach. Salsa uses abstract interpretation to bound maximum absolute error, producing a sound overapproximation of the maximum error. Herbie, on the other hand, uses random sampling to achieve a tight statistical approximation of bits error. The tight estimates enabled by statistical techniques provide additional opportunities for Herbie to improve the accuracy of an expression, but prevent it from providing sound error bounds. Finally, STOKE uses stochastic search to optimize floating-point programs, and must compare the accuracy of floating-point programs to avoid significantly compromising their accuracy. STOKE uses a Markov-chain Monte Carlo sampling to statistically evaluate maximum ULPs error.

By exactly describing the way each tool measures accuracy, FPBench makes it possible to compare and relate tools. Unsound tools such as Herbie or STOKE can be composed with a sound verification tool to produce an accuracy guarantee, and this guarantee can be compared to the approximate error measurements those tools made statistically. Since Fluctuat, FPTaylor, Rosa, and Salsa all soundly measure maximum forward absolute error, they can be compared to determine which technique is best.

4   Tools

FPBench features a collection of compilers and measurement tools that operates in its common format, FPCore. These tools can be a community resource, increasing interoperability as well as code reuse. They also make it easier to write new floating-point analysis and transformation tools by automating what are currently common but tedious tasks.

FPImp to FPCore. The FPCore format faithfully preserves important program constructs, such as variable binding and operation ordering, while abstracting away details not relevant to floating-point semantics. However, it is syntactically very different from some of the languages from which benchmarks might originate. To make translation to FPCore from source languages like C, Fortran, and

Matlab easier, FPBench provides the FPImp format and a compiler from FPImp to FPCore. FPImp is syntactically similar to imperative languages to make it easy to translate benchmarks.

FPCore to C. Since C is a common implementation language for mathematical computations, FPBench provides a FPCore to C compiler. The FPCore to C compiler can be used to run FPCore benchmarks through the many available C analysis tools.

Average error estimation. FPBench provides a tool to statistically approximate average error using naive sampling. The statistical approach is necessary to produce accurate estimates of average error given the current state of the art. The tool can use absolute, relative, ULPs, and bits error.

We plan to continue developing community tools around the FPBench formats, especially tools for estimating the other measures of error described in Sect. 3.

5   Benchmark Suite and Examples

The FPBench suite currently includes 44 benchmarks sourced from recent papers on automatic floating-point verification and accuracy improvement. This section first summarizes these benchmarks and then details how representative examples were translated to FPBench from the input formats of various tools in the literature.

The current FPBench suite contains examples from a variety of domains, including 28 from the Herbie test suite [21], 9 from the Salsa test suite [10], 7 from the Rosa test suite [11], and one example from the FPTaylor test suite [24]. These examples range from simple test programs for early tool development up to large examples for evaluating more mature tools. The larger examples are more challenging, including loops that with up to 13 variables mutated in the loop body. As shown in Tables 2 and 3, these programs exercise the full range of functionality available in FPBench, and span a variety application areas, from control software to mathematical libraries. We intend to continue adding benchmarks to the FPBench suite.

5.1   FPTaylor

FPTaylor [24] uses series expansions and interval arithmetic to compute sound error bounds. The authors gave the following simple program as an example input for their tool:

```
1: Variables
2:    float64  x  in  [1.001,  2.0],
3:    float64  y  in  [1.001,  2.0];
4: Definitions
5:    t rnd64= x * y;
6: Expressions
7:    r rnd64= (t-1)/(t*t-1);
```

Table 2. Functions and language features used in the FPBench benchmarks. Benchmarks contain a variety of features, and many benchmarks incorporate several. Exponential functions include logarithms, the exponential function, and the power function.

Table 3. Domains which the FPBench benchmarks are drawn from. Most are general mathematical operations, useful in a variety of domains. The general expressions are the smallest, and are drawn from *Numerical Methods for Scientists and Engineers* [16] and Rosa [11].

Feature	Benchmarks
Basic arithmetic	44
Exponentials	13
Trigonometric	10
Comparison	12
Loops	12
Conditionals	3

Domain	Benchmarks
General expressions	31
Math algorithms	6
Embedded systems	4
Scientific computing	3

This program is representative of the code necessary to correct sensor data in control software, where the output of the sensor is known to be between 1.001 and 2.0. We manually translated this program to FPCore, yielding:

```
(FPCore (x y)
  :name"FPTaylor example"
  :cite (solovyev-et-al-2015)
  :type binary64
  :pre (and (and (< 1.001 x) (< x 2.0)) (and (< 1.001 y) (< y 2.0)))
  (let ([t (* x y)])
    (/ (- t 1.0) (- (* t t) 1.0)))))
```

The benchmark takes inputs x and y and uses a `let` statement to represent the intermediate variables from the FPTaylor example. FPCore faithfully preserves important program constructs, such as variable binding and operation ordering, making the translation a simple matter. The benchmark additionally specifies a name and cites its source using a key to a standard BibTEX file. Since the original program uses 64-bit floating-point numbers, the type `binary64` is specified in the benchmark. The constraints on input variables are translated to a single predicate under the `:pre` property.

5.2 Rosa

Rosa [11] soundly verifies error bounds of floating-point programs, including looping control flow through recursive function calls. Several benchmarks in its repository demonstrate this capability, including one that uses Newton's method on a series representation of the sine function. In Rosa's input language the original benchmark is represented as:

```
def newton(x: Real, k: LoopCounter): Real = {
  require(-1.0 < x && x < 1.0)
  if (k < 10) {
    newton(x - (x - (x**3)/6.0 + (x**5)/120.0 + (x**7)/5040.0) /
      (1.0 - (x*x)/2.0 + (x**4)/24.0 + (x**6)/720.0), k++)
  } else {
    x
  }
} ensuring(res => -1.0 < res && res < 1.0)
```

The **require** clause denotes input preconditions, and the **ensures** clause provides the error bound to be verified. We manually translated this program to FPCore, yielding:

```
(FPCore (x0)
  :name ''Rosa Example"
  :cite (darulova-kuncak-2014)
  :pre (and (< -1.0 x0) (< x0 1.0))
  :rosa-post (and (< -1.0 RES) (< RES 1.0))
  (while (< i 10)
    ([i 0 (+ i 1)]
     [x x0
      (let ([f (+ (+ (- x (/ (pow x 3) 6))
                     (/ (pow x 5) 120)) (/ (pow x 7) 5040))]
            [df (+ (+ (- 1.0 (/ (* x x) 2))
                      (/ (pow x 4) 24)) (/ (pow x 6) 720))])
        (- x (/ f df)))])
    x))
```

Like the FPTaylor benchmark, this benchmark includes a name, citation for its source, and precondition on inputs. For completeness, we've also included the **ensuring** annotation, denoted :rosa-post, demonstrating the ability to add tool specific annotations by prefixing with the tool name. Note how the **while** construct from FPCore can be used to represent the tail-recursive loop from the Rosa original benchmark.

5.3 Herbie

Herbie [21] heuristically improves the accuracy of straight-line floating-point expressions. The authors demonstrate the improvements Herbie can produce using the quadratic formula for computing the roots of a second degree polynomial. It has uses from calculating trajectories to solving matrix equations. In mathematical notation, the quadratic formula is given by:[6]

$$\frac{(-b) - \sqrt{b^2 - 4ac}}{2a}$$

Herbie produces the following more-accurate variant:

$$\begin{cases} \frac{4ac}{-b+\sqrt{b^2-4ac}}/2a & \text{if } b < 0 \\ \left(-b - \sqrt{b^2 - 4ac}\right)\frac{1}{2a} & \text{if } 0 \le b \le 10^{127} \\ -\frac{b}{a} + \frac{c}{b} & \text{if } 10^{127} < b \end{cases}$$

---

[6] We use the negative variant here, as in the Herbie paper; the positive variant is analogous.

In FPCore format, the original formula is represented as:

```
(FPCore (a b c)
  :name ''NMSE p42, positive''
  :cite (hamming−1987)
  :pre (and (>= (sqr b) (* 4 (* a c))) (!= a 0))
  (/ (+ (− b) (sqrt (− (sqr b) (* 4 (* a c))))) (* 2 a)))
```

and the improved version is represented as:

```
(FPCore (a b c)
  :name ''NMSE p42, positive''
  :cite (hamming−1987)
  :pre (and (>= (sqr b) (* 4 (* a c))) (!= a 0))
  (if (< b 0)
      (/ (/ (* 4 (* a c)) (+ (− b) (sqrt (− (sqr b) (* 4 (* a c)))))))
         (* 2 a))
      (if (< b 10e127)
          (* (− (− b) (− (sqr b) (* 4 (* a c)))) (/ 1 (* 2 a)))
          (+ (− (/ b a)) (/ c b)))))
```

Like the Rosa and FPTaylor examples, this benchmark gives a name, citation, and precondition. This benchmark uses FPCore's ability to write arbitrary boolean expressions as preconditions, restricting the value under the square root to be non-negative and requiring the denominator be non-zero. Unlike the FPTaylor and Rosa examples, this precondition arises from mathematical considerations, not domain knowledge. The FPCore version of Herbie's output furthermore uses if constructs to evaluate different expressions for different inputs, which improves accuracy. Herbie could add additional metadata to the output, such as its internal estimate of accuracy or the number of expressions considered during search, by using prefixed keys like :herbie-accuracy-estimate.

5.4   Salsa

Salsa [10] is a tool for soundly improving the worst-case accuracy of programs. The authors evaluate Salsa on a suite of control and numerical algorithms, including the widely used PID controller algorithm. This algorithm is used in aeronautic and avionic systems for which correctness is critical. In C, the benchmark is written as:

```
volatile double p, i, t, d, dt, invdt, m, e, eold, r;
int pid(double m0, double kp, double ki, double kd, double c){
    t     = 0.0;
    invdt = 5.0;
    dt    = 0.2;
    m     = m0 ;
    eold  = 0.0;
    i     = 0.0;
    while (t < 100.0) {
        e = c − m;
        p = kp * e;
        i = i + ki * dt * e;
        d = kd * invdt * (e − eold);
        r = p + i + d;
        m = m + 0.01 * r; /* computing measure: the plant */
        eold = e;
        t = t + dt;
    }
    return m;
}
```

To ease the conversion of this code from C to FPCore, this program was first manually translated to the following FPImp program:

```
(FPImp (m kp ki kd)
 :name ''PID''
 :description ''Keep a measure at its setpoint using a PID controller.''
 :cite (damouche−martel−chapoutot−nsv14)
 :type binary64
 :pre (and (and (< −10.0 m) (< m 10.0)) (and (< −10.0 c) (< c 10.0)))
 [= t 0.0]
 [= dt 0.2]
 [= invdt (/ 1 dt)]
 [= c 0.0]
 [= eold 0.0]
 [= i 0.0]
 (while (< t 100.0)
    [= e (− c m)]
    [= p (* kp e)]
    [= i (+ i (* (* ki dt) e))]
    [= d (* (* kd invdt) (− e eold))]
    [= r (+ (+ p i) d)]
    [= m (+ m (* 0.01 r))]
    [= eold e]
    [= t (+ t dt)])
 (output m))
```

The FPImp program was then automatically compiled, using the compiler tool in FPBench, to the following FPCore benchmark:

```
(FPCore (m0 kp ki kd c)
 :name ''PID"
 :description "Keep a measure at its setpoint using a PID controller."
 :cite (damouche−martel−chapoutot−nsv14)
 :type binary64
 :pre (and (and (< −10.0 m0) (< m0 10.0)) (and (< −10.0 c) (< c 10.0)))
 (while (< t 100.0)
    ([i 0.0 (+ i (* (* ki 0.2) (− c m)))]
     [m m0
        (let ([p (* kp (− c m))]
              [d (* (* kd (/ 1 0.2)) (− (− c m) eold))])
          (+ m (* 0.01 (+ (+ p (+ i (* (* ki 0.2) (− c m)))) d))))]
     [eold 0.0 (− c m)]
     [t 0.0 (+ t 0.2)])
    m))
```

Beyond the metadata used in the FPTaylor, Rosa, and Herbie examples, this benchmark includes a :description tag to describe for readers what the benchmark program computes. These descriptions contain information about the distribution of inputs, the situation in which the benchmark is used, or any other information which might be useful to tool writers. The FPBench suite features descriptions for its most complex benchmarks.

6   Conclusion

The initial work on FPBench provides a foundation for evaluating and comparing floating-point analysis and optimization tools. Already the FPBench format can serve as a common language, allowing these tools to cooperatively analyze and improve floating-point code.

Though FPBench supports the composition of the floating-point tools that exist today, there is still much work to do to support the floating-point research community as it grows. FPBench must be sufficiently expressive for the broad range of applications that represent the future of the community. In the near term, we will add additional metrics for accuracy and performance to the set of evaluators provided by the FPBench tooling and begin developing a standard set of benchmarks around the various measures. We will also expand the set of languages with direct support for compilation to and from the FPBench format. As more tools grow support for FPBench, we will provide automated comparisons of different floating-point tools. Longer term, we intend to support for mixed-precision benchmarks, fixed-point computations, and additional data structures such as vectors, records, and matrices.

We hope that FPBench encourages the already strong sense of community and collaboration around floating-point research. Toward that end, we encourage any interested readers (and tool writers) to get involved with development of FPBench by signing up for the mailing list and checking out the project website: http://fpbench.org/.

References

1. DIMACS challenge. Satisfiability. Suggested format (1993). http://www.cs.ubc.ca/~hoos/SATLIB/Benchmarks/SAT/satformat.ps
2. Adjé, A., Garoche, P.-L., Werey, A.: Quadratic zonotopes. In: Feng, X., Park, S. (eds.) APLAS 2015. LNCS, vol. 9458, pp. 127–145. Springer, Cham (2015). doi:10.1007/978-3-319-26529-2_8
3. Barrett, C., Fontaine, P., Tinelli, C.: The SMT-LIB Standard: Version 2.5. Technical report, Department of Computer Science, The University of Iowa (2015). www.SMT-LIB.org
4. Bertrane, J., Cousot, P., Cousot, R., Feret, J., Mauborgne, L., Miné, A., Rival, X.: Static analysis and verification of aerospace software by abstract interpretation. Found. Trends Program. Lang. 2(2–3), 71–190 (2015)
5. Bessey, A., Block, K., Chelf, B., Chou, A., Fulton, B., Hallem, S., Henri-Gros, C., Kamsky, A., McPeak, S., Engler, D.: A few billion lines of code later: using static analysis to find bugs in the real world. Commun. ACM 53(2), 66–75 (2010)
6. Cadar, C., Dunbar, D., Engler, D.: Klee: unassisted and automatic generation of high-coverage tests for complex systems programs. In: Proceedings of the 8th USENIX Conference on Operating Systems Design and Implementation (OSDI 2008), Berkeley, CA, USA, pp. 209–224. USENIX Association (2008)
7. Chapoutot, A.: Interval slopes as a numerical abstract domain for floating-point variables. In: Cousot, R., Martel, M. (eds.) SAS 2010. LNCS, vol. 6337, pp. 184–200. Springer, Heidelberg (2010). doi:10.1007/978-3-642-15769-1_12
8. Clarke, E., Kroening, D., Lerda, F.: A tool for checking ANSI-C programs. In: Jensen, K., Podelski, A. (eds.) TACAS 2004. LNCS, vol. 2988, pp. 168–176. Springer, Heidelberg (2004). doi:10.1007/978-3-540-24730-2_15
9. Cousot, P., Cousot, R.: Abstract interpretation frameworks. J. Log. Comput. 2(4), 511–547 (1992)
10. Damouche, N., Martel, M., Chapoutot, A.: Intra-procedural optimization of the numerical accuracy of programs. In: Núñez, M., Güdemann, M. (eds.) FMICS 2015. LNCS, vol. 9128, pp. 31–46. Springer, Cham (2015). doi:10.1007/978-3-319-19458-5_3

11. Darulova, E., Kuncak, V.: Sound compilation of reals. In: Jagannathan, S., Sewell, P., (eds.), POPL 2014, pp. 235–248. ACM (2014)
12. Goubault, E.: Static analysis by abstract interpretation of numerical programs and systems, and FLUCTUAT. In: Logozzo, F., Fähndrich, M. (eds.) SAS 2013. LNCS, vol. 7935, pp. 1–3. Springer, Heidelberg (2013). doi:10.1007/978-3-642-38856-9_1
13. Goubault, E., Martel, M., Putot, S.: Some future challenges in the validation of control systems. In: European Congress on Embedded Real Time Software (ERTS 2006), Proceedings (2006)
14. Goubault, E., Putot, S.: Static analysis of finite precision computations. In: Jhala, R., Schmidt, D. (eds.) VMCAI 2011. LNCS, vol. 6538, pp. 232–247. Springer, Heidelberg (2011). doi:10.1007/978-3-642-18275-4_17
15. Griewank, A., Walther, A.: Evaluating derivatives - principles and techniques of algorithmic differentiation (2 ed.). SIAM (2008)
16. Hamming, R.: Numerical Methods for Scientists and Engineers, 2nd edn. Dover Publications, New York (1987)
17. Henning, J.L.: SPEC CPU2006 benchmark descriptions. SIGARCH Comput. Archit. News **34**(4), 1–17 (2006)
18. Holzmann, G.J.: Mars code. Commun. ACM **57**(2), 64–73 (2014)
19. Lee, W., Sharma, R., Aiken, A.: Verifying bit-manipulations of floating-point. In: Proceedings of the 37th ACM SIGPLAN Conference on Programming Language Design and Implementation (PLDI 2016), New York, NY, USA. ACM (2016)
20. Martel, M.: An overview of semantics for the validation of numerical programs. In: Cousot, R. (ed.) VMCAI 2005. LNCS, vol. 3385, pp. 59–77. Springer, Heidelberg (2005). doi:10.1007/978-3-540-30579-8_4
21. Wilcox, J.-R., Panchekha, P., Sanchez-Stern, A., Tatlock, Z.: Automatically improving accuracy for floating point expressions. In: Grove, D., Blackburn, S., (eds.), PLDI 2015, pp. 1–11. ACM (2015)
22. Sankaranarayanan, S.: Static analysis in the continuously changing world. In: Logozzo, F., Fähndrich, M. (eds.) SAS 2013. LNCS, vol. 7935, pp. 4–5. Springer, Heidelberg (2013). doi:10.1007/978-3-642-38856-9_2
23. Schkufza, E., Sharma, R., Aiken, A.: Stochastic optimization of floating-point programs with tunable precision. In: Proceedings of the 35th ACM SIGPLAN Conference on Programming Language Design and Implementation (PLDI 2014), New York, NY, USA. ACM (2014)
24. Solovyev, A., Jacobsen, C., Rakamarić, Z., Gopalakrishnan, G.: Rigorous estimation of floating-point round-off errors with symbolic taylor expansions. In: Bjørner, N., de Boer, F. (eds.) FM 2015: Formal Methods. Programming and Software Engineering, vol. 9109. Springer, Heidelberg (2015)
25. Woo, S.C., Ohara, M., Torrie, E., Singh, J.P., Gupta, A.: The SPLASH-2 programs: characterization and methodological considerations. In: Proceedings of the 22nd Annual International Symposium on Computer Architecture (ISCA 1995), pp. 24–36, New York, NY, USA. ACM (1995)

Falsification of Dynamical Systems –
An Industrial Perspective

Thomas Heinz[✉]

Robert-Bosch GmbH, Corporate Research,
Robert-Bosch-Campus 1, 71272 Renningen, Germany
thomas.heinz@de.bosch.com

Abstract. Whenever formal verification of dynamical system models is not applicable, e.g., due to the presence of black-box components, simulation-based verification and falsification methods are promising approaches to gain confidence in a system satisfying its specification. With the introduction of robust semantics it is not only possible to answer this question in the Boolean sense but to quantify its truth. We illustrate a number of applications that are interesting from an industrial perspective, and point out how robustness could become even more versatile in the engineering process.

Keywords: Falsification · Conformance · Testing · Robust semantics · Simulation-based verification · Automotive control systems

1 Introduction

Models of dynamical systems play a crucial role in the development of automotive control systems. Here, we focus on models describing the closed-loop interaction between physical processes and controllers. Such models exist at various levels of abstraction, e.g., in order to design a controller, a simplified physical model is used whereas for validation purposes the controller is tested against a detailed physical model. Controller models on the other hand range from abstract continuous-time models to fixed-step implementation models involving precise digital hardware behavior. There exist a variety of different modeling tools specialized in different physics domains based on different formalisms such as PDEs (partial differential equations), ODEs (ordinary differential equations), DAEs (differential algebraic equations), and hybrid or switched versions thereof. The situation is similar for controller models. Modeling tools such as Matlab/Simulink or Modelica can express both physics and high-level continuous- or discrete-time controllers in a single model. During refinement of the controller implementation however, different tools must be used that reflect real-time scheduling [9], and hardware behavior as well. Co-simulation is required

---

T. Heinz Invited talk. Thanks to my colleagues Jens Oehlerking, Matthias Woehrle, and Christoph Gladisch for valuable discussions and feedback.

S. Bogomolov et al. (Eds.): NSV 2016, LNCS 10152, pp. 78–84, 2017.
DOI: 10.1007/978-3-319-54292-8_7

to perform closed-loop simulations of such implementation models and physical processes, i.e., the entire system model is represented by different modeling tools and the simulation becomes a distributed process which is typically coordinated by a single tool. Alternatively, tool-specific models are converted into tool-independent models such as FMUs (Functional Mock-up Units) [3]. Given the current state of the art, it is not possible to formally verify functional properties of such models. This is partially due to the lack of formal semantics of some modeling tools and the presence of black-box components in form of libraries. For physical processes which do not admit an appropriate characterization by closed-form ODE/DAE models, such as combustion, the model may involve functions described by large tables of data. In these cases, even if we describe the model in a mathematically unambiguous way, e.g., as a hybrid automaton, formal verification such as reachability analysis is often not practically possible with state of the art methods.

A promising approach to address these complexities is simulation-based verification resp. falsification built on top of robust semantics for temporal property specification logics [7, 8]. So far research has mostly focused on variants of linear temporal logic (LTL), in particular metric temporal logic (MTL) and signal temporal logic (STL). The basic idea is to generalize the Boolean semantics of a temporal logic by a metric. In the Boolean semantics, a signal (trace) either satisfies a specification or not. In a robust semantics, a signal is mapped to a real number indicating some measure of distance to the satisfaction "border". A value in $\mathbb{R}_0^+$ indicates that the signal satisfies the specification, a value in $\mathbb{R}^-$ shows that it does not. Such a quantification of truth enables the use of optimization methods to guide the exploration of a model and to find initial conditions, parameters, and possible input signals falsifying the property. If the model indeed satisfies the property – which is in general undecidable – the exploration tries to minimize the degree of satisfaction. Under certain assumptions, e.g., the model being Lipschitz continuous, simulation-based verification is possible, i.e., a finite number of simulation runs may suffice to show a temporal property [6]. In the following, these approaches are summarized by the term *property conformance checking*.

During model refinement from abstract to implementation models, it is important to preserve desired properties. Property conformance checking is a way to increase confidence in this preservation. Besides satisfying particular properties, it is often desirable that the behavior of a refined system is close to that of the original system, e.g., when the physics model is replaced by a more complex one or when disturbances are introduced. Another example is comparing a continuous-time model with a discrete-time version with delays characterizing timing properties of the distributed execution of the controller such as computation, communication, and scheduling delays. It has been observed that equivalence notions from discrete systems such as bisimilarity are too strong to adequately capture similarity of closed-loop control models. Instead, quantifying the distance of pairs of corresponding signals from both models provides a useful indication of model similarity. Deshmukh et al. [5] introduce an effective method to compute the distance of signals under the Skorokhod metric which considers retimed versions $s(r(t))$ of a signal $s(t)$ with r being a monotonically increasing retiming function. The idea is to capture both distortions in space and time where time distortions can be more general than constant time shifts. Subsequently, this approach is called *model conformance checking*.

2   Industrially Relevant Applications

Automatic testing is important in industrial practice to have high confidence that the product meets its requirements when formal methods are not applicable. Tests capturing property or model conformance on the level of "virtual" models are already useful as indicated above. Testing the real system is inevitable even if the entire chain of model refinements would be formally verified. This is expensive compared to simulations and thus benefits from careful selection of relevant test cases, i.e., those which either falsify the property, or operate the system at the satisfiability limit. In the context of vehicle dynamics, such test cases can be executed from driving robots which control steering, acceleration, and braking [11]. In the realm of automated driving, a test case may be as complex as finding a particular challenging road configuration with potential obstacles, and defining the behavior of dynamic objects other than the automated vehicle itself.

Clearly, it is desirable to have models which admit **formal verification in practice**. A formal model could be used to describe the behavior for a subset of outputs, e.g., a Büchi automaton capturing discrete behavior. Alternatively, it may be a simplified dynamics model such as a system of ODEs or a linear hybrid automaton, which presumably overapproximates the behavior in a subset of the original state space, hence enabling reachability analysis [2,10] and theorem proving [12]. Model conformance checking can provide best effort indication that a formal model is indeed an abstraction of the original system.

Property conformance checking as described above computes a single robustness value for a particular signal, and thus quantifies the satisfaction of the property by that signal. **Online monitoring** is a form of property conformance checking where a robustness signal is computed, i.e., a function mapping each signal prefix to its robustness value [4]. A robustness signal provides valuable feedback for developers in understanding how the satisfaction of a property evolves in time. Moreover, if the monitor can be computed in real-time, its output could be used to modify the system behavior, e.g., in case a system is approaching its satisfiability limit, it could activate some fallback behavior before the property is actually violated.

A black-box model contains inputs, outputs, parameters and states. In practice, it is often not possible to know all states as they might be hidden in libraries that are part of the model. For autonomous models, i.e., ones without input, property or model conformance checking explores a given parameter space. If inputs are present, the exploration problem becomes more involved. A simple approach is to select inputs from a predefined family of input functions. The disadvantage is that the relation of input to state space is unknown. Consider the simple property $\Box(x \geq 2 \Rightarrow \Diamond_{[0,1]} y \leq 3)$ where x is a state, and y an output. If the goal is to select an interesting input, it would have to be such that $x \geq 2$ holds eventually. Selecting inputs from a predefined set works only if the set is carefully chosen with knowledge about the model that must be obtained by other means. Another approach would be to simply set $x_0 \geq 2$ initially but this is not possible when the test is performed on a real system as we can obviously not simply set real physical states in this way. Hence, for this practically relevant class of specifications, test generation involves **control synthesis**. There are numerous publications about this subject such as [13] which constructs a receding horizon controller from an STL specification. However, it is not clear how to deal with hidden states. Moreover, constraints on inputs must be respected to avoid damaging the real system under test.

Scenario-based verification is an important first step in mastering the safety challenge for automated driving. Instead of testing many individual scenarios, formal specification languages may provide an effective way of producing families of non-deterministic driving scenarios and expectations from the automated vehicle therein. STL – while being amenable to efficient online monitoring – might not be convenient or expressive enough because it is not possible to refer to previous signal values at a given point in time. Introducing the so-called freeze operator [4] solves this problem but at the cost of online monitoring becoming more expensive.

3   One Robustness Does Not Fit All

Property conformance checking as described in Sect. 1 is key to various industrially relevant applications sketched above. The notion of robustness generalizes the classical Boolean semantics by quantifying the satisfaction of a temporal property. Initially, space robustness [8] was proposed to measure the satisfaction degree of a signal with respect to a formula. The robustness value indicates how much the entire signal can be shifted in space and still satisfy the formula. Most publications dealing with robust semantics of temporal logics are based on space robustness. As a generalization, space-time robustness [7] was introduced where time robustness describes how much a signal may be shifted in time and still satisfy the formula. Besides various semantics, an STL extension was proposed which augments the logic by two operators (averaged-until and averaged-released) [1]. The metric associated with these operators allows to express for example expeditiousness, persistence (as long as possible), and soft deadlines (earlier is better).

In practice, the properties of a model can often be written in the form $\Box \bigwedge_{1 \leq i \leq n}(\phi_i \Rightarrow \psi_i)$ where ϕ_i refers to inputs and states and ψ_i refers to inputs and outputs. A single notion of robustness is not sufficient to represent the property adequately. For a test/simulation to be relevant, it is required that some ϕ_i is satisfied since otherwise the formula holds trivially. While it is possible that the precondition benefits from robust semantics, it may as well be sufficient to

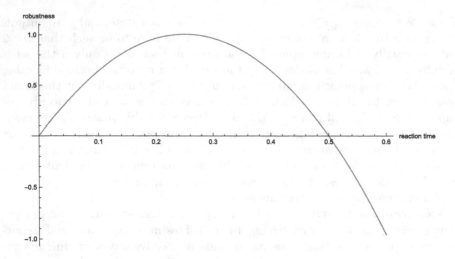

Fig. 1. Robustness for acceleration pedal reaction

evaluate the precondition under the Boolean semantics. For different postconditions though, different robustness metrics might be desirable. Let

$$\phi_1 \equiv \phi_2 \equiv input\_step$$
$$\psi_1 \equiv \square_{[0,10]} x \leq 1.2$$
$$\psi_2 \equiv \psi_{2,1} \wedge \psi_{2,2}$$
$$\psi_{2,1} \equiv \square_{[0,13]} \; input\_unchanged$$
$$\psi_{2,2} \equiv \lozenge_{[0,3]} \square_{[0,10]} 0.98 \leq x \leq 1.02$$

where $\phi_1 \Rightarrow \psi_1$ is an overshoot and $\phi_2 \Rightarrow \psi_2$ is a settling time requirement. It is natural to evaluate ψ_1 under the space robustness semantics (less overshoot is better), $\psi_{2,1}$ under the Boolean semantics (input should not change), and $\psi_{2,2}$ under the time robustness semantics (earlier settling is better). The robustness of the entire requirement can be computed by suitable monitors for the subformulas from which a single robustness value can be calculated. This is possible whenever the formula can be structurally decomposed into parts such that each part can be assigned any of the standard robustness metrics. However, faster/earlier is not always better, neither is slower/later. Consider a simplified requirement for an accelerator pedal.

$$\phi \equiv pedal\_pushed$$
$$\psi \equiv \lozenge_{[0,0.5]} a \geq 1$$

Figure 1 illustrates a robustness definition which favors neither fast nor slow reaction time but defines the optimal reaction time to be at 0.25 s with robustness 1. Recall that a non-negative value indicates satisfaction, and a negative value indicates violation of the property. Deviations from the optimal reaction time are penalized symmetrically, i.e., $0 \leq r(0.25 + \Delta) = r(0.25 - \Delta) \leq 1$, $\Delta \in [0, 0.25]$ where $r(t)$ denotes the robustness of reaction time t. Reaction times greater than 0.5 s violate the property and its negative robustness grows quadratically with increasing reaction time. Such a robustness is not conveniently expressible as time robustness in the sense mentioned above. It would be possible to approximate this notion arbitrarily by dividing the interval [0, 0.5] into subintervals each associated with time robustness, and then compute the overall robustness from the robustness values associated with each time interval. However, such a specification is neither convenient nor precise.

The notion of robust semantics for temporal logics is very powerful. MTL/STL offer great flexibility in specifying non-trivial properties. A similar degree of freedom for specifying metrics would be of great value. Ideally, a developer would be able to define both the property and a suitable metric. The metric differentiates between good and bad signals among all those which satisfy the specification in the Boolean sense. This allows an intuitive understanding of the robustness signal and enables meaningful computation involving different robustness values. Besides assisting engineers in assessing the quality of their models, metric diversity may be useful in steering the optimization process into different regions of the state space.

4   Conclusion

Property and model conformance checking are versatile approaches to assess correctness of industrial models that cannot be handled by current state of the art formal methods due black-box components and other complexities. By quantifying the degree to which a property is satisfied based on recently introduced robust semantics of linear temporal logics, it is possible to effectively explore models and discover property violating behavior, or behavior which is close to the satisfaction "border". In practice however, one particular robust semantics cannot adequately capture all desired quantifications of truth. Thus, we encourage to develop a generalized robust semantics which enables user-defined metrics, thus leveraging flexible and intuitive composition of multiple properties.

References

1. Akazaki, T., Hasuo, I.: Time robustness in MTL and expressivity in hybrid system falsification. In: Kroening, D., Păsăreanu, C.S. (eds.) CAV 2015. LNCS, vol. 9207, pp. 356–374. Springer, Cham (2015). doi:10.1007/978-3-319-21668-3_21
2. Althoff, M.: An introduction to CORA 2015. In: Proceedings of the Workshop on Applied Verification for Continuous and Hybrid Systems (2015)
3. Bastian, J., Clauß, C., Wolf, S., Schneider, P.: Master for co-simulation using FMI. In: 8th International Modelica Conference, Dresden. Citeseer (2011)
4. Deshmukh, J.V., Donzé, A., Ghosh, S., Jin, X., Juniwal, G., Seshia, S.A.: Robust online monitoring of signal temporal logic. In: Bartocci, E., Majumdar, R. (eds.) RV 2015. LNCS, vol. 9333, pp. 55–70. Springer, Cham (2015). doi:10.1007/978-3-319-23820-3_4

5. Deshmukh, J.V., Majumdar, R., Prabhu, V.S.: Quantifying conformance using the Skorokhod metric. In: Kroening, D., Păsăreanu, C.S. (eds.) CAV 2015. LNCS, vol. 9207, pp. 234–250. Springer, Cham (2015). doi:10.1007/978-3-319-21668-3_14

6. Donzé, A., Maler, O.: Systematic simulation using sensitivity analysis. In: Bemporad, A., Bicchi, A., Buttazzo, G. (eds.) HSCC 2007. LNCS, vol. 4416, pp. 174–189. Springer, Heidelberg (2007). doi:10.1007/978-3-540-71493-4_16

7. Donzé, A., Maler, O.: Robust satisfaction of temporal logic over real-valued signals. In: Chatterjee, K., Henzinger, T.A. (eds.) FORMATS 2010. LNCS, vol. 6246, pp. 92–106. Springer, Heidelberg (2010). doi:10.1007/978-3-642-15297-9_9

8. Fainekos, G.E., Pappas, G.J.: Robustness of temporal logic specifications for continuous-time signals. Theoret. Comput. Sci. **410**(42), 4262–4291 (2009)

9. Frehse, G., Hamann, A., Quinton, S., Woehrle, M.: Formal analysis of timing effects on closed-loop properties of control software. In: 2014 IEEE on Real-Time Systems Symposium (RTSS), pp. 53–62. IEEE (2014)

10. Immler, F.: Verified reachability analysis of continuous systems. In: Baier, C., Tinelli, C. (eds.) TACAS 2015. LNCS, vol. 9035, pp. 37–51. Springer, Heidelberg (2015). doi:10.1007/978-3-662-46681-0_3

11. Mikesell, D.R.: Portable automated driver for universal road vehicle dynamics testing. Ph.D. thesis, The Ohio State University (2008)

12. Platzer, A.: Logical Analysis of Hybrid Systems: Proving Theorems for Complex Dynamics. Springer, Heidelberg (2010)

13. Raman, V., Donzé, A., Maasoumy, M., Murray, R.M., Sangiovanni-Vincentelli, A., Seshia, S.A.: Model predictive control with signal temporal logic specifications. In: 2014 IEEE 53rd Annual Conference on Decision and Control (CDC), pp. 81–87. IEEE (2014)

Model Based Automatic Code Generation
for Nonlinear Model Predictive Control

Behzad Samadi$^{(\boxtimes)}$

Maplesoft, Waterloo, ON, Canada
bsamadi@maplesoft.com

Abstract. This paper demonstrates a symbolic tool that generates
C code for nonlinear model predictive controllers. The optimality conditions are derived in a quick tutorial on optimal control. A model based
workflow using MapleSim for modeling and simulation, and Maple for
analysis and code generation is then explained. In this paper, we assume
to have a control model of a nonlinear plant in MapleSim. The first
step of the workflow is to get the equations of the control model from
MapleSim. These equations are usually in the form of differential algebraic equations. After converting the equations to ordinary differential
equations, the C code for the model predictive controller is generated
using a tool created in Maple. The resulting C code can be used to
simulate the control algorithm and program the hardware controller.
The proposed tool for automatic code generation for model predictive
controllers is open and can be employed by users to create their own
customized code generation tool.

Keywords: Model predictive control · Code generation · Model based

1 Introduction

A systematic workflow for model based automatic code generation for Model
Predictive Control (MPC) is introduced in this paper (Fig. 1). MPC started as
the alternative advanced control method to PID controllers in chemical process
industries. With the progress of MPC algorithms and the computational power
of hardware controllers, other industries such as the robotics, automotive and
aerospace industries are looking into MPC controllers. The majority of current
MPC controllers use linear models because in that case, the controller needs
to solve a Quadratic Programming (QP), which is a convex optimization problem that can be solved efficiently. However, linear models are not adequate for
highly nonlinear systems. MPC controller synthesis based on physical modeling is the approach that can be employed to overcome the inefficiency of linear
models. Working with physical models is on the other hand not easy. Control
engineers need high-level modeling tools to save time, improve reliability and
prevent human error getting into the controller code.

MapleSim [1], as an advanced high-level tool for physical modeling and simulation, and Maple [2], as an advanced symbolic analysis and synthesis tool, are

© Springer International Publishing AG 2017
S. Bogomolov et al. (Eds.): NSV 2016, LNCS 10152, pp. 85–95, 2017.
DOI: 10.1007/978-3-319-54292-8_8

natural building blocks of the proposed workflow for automatic code generation for MPC. The workflow, depicted in Fig. 1, consists of the following steps:

- *Modeling:* A physical model of the system is built by connecting components in MapleSim. MapleSim contains more than 550 built-in components from many different domains. Users can also create their own custom components.
- *Extracting the equations:* The dynamic equations of this model are then extracted into Maple. In general, automatically generated dynamic equations of a physical model are in the form of differential algebraic equations (DAE).
- *Converting DAEs to ODEs:* Most MPC algorithms assume that the equations are given in the form of ordinary differential equations (ODE). Maple is employed in the workflow to convert DAEs to ODEs. The conversion can be exact or an approximation in order to simplify the resulting ODEs. Currently, this step is not systematic and it may be different for each system.
- *Generating Code:* The MPC algorithm for the given the ODE equations can be generated using Maple's symbolic computation engine. The resulting Maple code can be converted to C code automatically using the CodeGeneration package.
- *Simulating the Closed Loop System:* The generated C code can be embedded in a MapleSim model as an External C Block. The closed loop system with the original DAE equations can then be simulated in MapleSim.

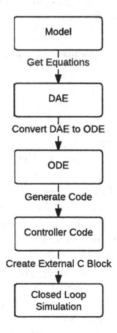

Fig. 1. Model-based automatic code Generation for MPC

An MPC controller consists of two main parts: problem formulation and the solver. Both of these parts can be generated in Maple and then translated to C code. In the Sect. 2, we will explain the approach we have followed to design an MPC controller. Mathematical details of the approach are described in Sect. 3. As an example, a system with electrical, mechanical and hydraulic components is considered in Sect. 4. The importance of this example is that it demonstrates automatic generation of dynamic equations, MPC problem formulation and an MPC solver. Corresponding MapleSim models and Maple worksheets will be provided to interested readers upon request.

2   Model Predictive Control

Consider a driver on a road. For a safe trip, the driver needs to look forward (prediction), follow the road and avoid any collision (constraints). On top of that, the driver might want to spend as little time and fuel as possible to reach the destination (optimization).

MPC can be employed to drive a self-driving car. The MPC controller minimizes a cost function at each time instant. Some of the optimization constraints that should be respected are listed below:

- Vehicle's dynamic behavior
- Limited power
- No skidding
- Following the road
- Avoiding collision

MPC is in fact a control method that computes the control input of the system by solving an Optimal Control Problem (OCP) in real time. The aim of the OCP is to optimize the trajectory of the system with respect to a cost function that is defined based on economic or performance measures. An MPC controller uses a model of the system to predict its behavior within a finite horizon. The following steps describe what an MPC controller performs in real time:

1. Measure/estimate the current state.
2. Solve the OCP to compute a sequence of control inputs.
3. Apply the first step in the control input sequence to the system.
4. Go to step 1.

MPC controllers were originally developed to control chemical processes [3]. PID controllers have been common in process control for a long time. However, there are a few issues with using PID controllers:

- *Highly nonlinear systems:* PID controllers do not perform well for highly non-linear systems.

- *Multiple coupled loops:* To control a multi-input multi-output (MIMO) system, many PID controllers in different loops are required and it is hard to compensate the coupling effect.
- *Tuning:* Tuning PID controllers is not an easy task especially when there are limits on the control input.

MPC controllers have the following features:

- MPC can minimize a cost function defined based on economic or performance properties of the system.
- MPC can handle constraints on inputs and states.
- MPC can be designed for MIMO nonlinear systems.
- Tuning an MPC controller is more intuitive compared to a set of PID controllers.
- MPC is a systematic, model based approach.
- There are tools for generating code for MPC controllers automatically.

2.1 Applications

MPC was first employed to control chemical processes in 1970s. In a survey of industrial applications of MPC, reference [3] mentions thousands of applications in refining, petrochemicals, chemicals, pulp and paper, polymer and food processing industries. Chemical processes are usually very slow and expensive. Therefore, there is plenty of time and computational power available to the controller. The largest size for plants reported in [3] is 603 inputs and 283 outputs. The majority of the MPC controllers in process control use linear models for the plant. The main reason is that the OCP in an MPC controller for a linear system with constraints can be formulated as a Quadratic Programming (QP) problem. Even large QP problems can be solved efficiently.

For nonlinear systems, the OCP is a nonlinear optimization problem, which are hard to solve in general. In [4], it is stated that, in process control, the use of linear MPC decreases with increasing process nonlinearity. In recent years, computational power of microprocessors has increased and new algorithms have been proposed for implementing MPC controllers. The result has been very fast implementations of MPC and the increasing interest in robotics, automotive and aerospace industries to use MPC controllers.

3   Mathematical Description

Consider the following nonlinear system:

$$\dot{x}(t) = f(x(t), u(t))$$
$$x(t_0) = x_\circ$$

where:

- $x(t)$ is the state vector
- $u(t)$ is the input vector

The objective of the MPC controller is to solve the following OCP:

$$\underset{u}{\text{minimize}}\ J(x_0, t_0) = \phi(x(t_f)) + \int_{t_0}^{t_f} L(x(\tau), u(\tau))d\tau$$

$$\text{subject to } \dot{x}(t) = f(x(t), u(t))$$

$$x(t_0) = x_\circ$$

$$g_i(x(t), u(t)) = 0, \text{ for } i = 1, \ldots, n_g$$

$$h_i(x(t), u(t)) \le 0, \text{ for } i = 1, \ldots, n_h$$

This OCP is in general a nonconvex optimization problem and it is hard to solve. A particular *interior-point algorithm*, the *barrier method* [5], is employed here to convert the inequality constraints to equality constraints [6]:

$$\underset{u,\sigma}{\text{minimize}}\ \phi(x(t_f)) + \int_{t_0}^{t_f} \left(L(x(\tau), u(\tau)) - r^{\mathrm{T}}\sigma(\tau) \right) d\tau$$

$$\text{subject to } \dot{x}(t) = f(x(t), u(t))$$

$$x(t_0) = x_\circ$$

$$g_i(x(t), u(t)) = 0, \text{ for } i = 1, \ldots, n_g$$

$$h_i(x(t), u(t)) + \sigma_i(t)^2 = 0, \text{ for } i = 1, \ldots, n_h$$

where $\sigma(t) \in \mathbb{R}^{n_h}$ is a vector slack variable and the entries of $r \in \mathbb{R}^{n_h}$ are small positive numbers. The vector r is chosen by the user. To put more penalty on the solution when it gets close to $h_i(x(t), u(t)) = 0$, the user should increase the corresponding entry of r.

If the problem is discretized into N steps from t_0 to t_f, we have:

$$\underset{u,\sigma}{\text{minimize}}\ \phi_d(x_N) + \sum_{k=0}^{N-1} \left(L(x_k, u_k) - r^{\mathrm{T}}\sigma_k \right)$$

$$\text{subject to } x_{k+1} = f_d(x_k, u_k)$$

$$x_0 = x_\circ$$

$$g_i(x_k, u_k) = 0, \text{ for } i = 1, \ldots, n_g$$

$$h_i(x_k, u_k) + \sigma_{ik}^2 = 0, \text{ for } i = 1, \ldots, n_h$$

where $\Delta\tau = \frac{t_f - t_0}{N}$ and:

$$\phi_d(x_N) = \frac{\phi(x(t_f), t_f)}{\Delta\tau} \ .$$

$$f_d(x_k, u_k) = x_k + f(x_k, u_k)\Delta\tau$$

By putting all the equality constraints into a vector G, we have:

$$\underset{u,\sigma}{\text{minimize}} \ \phi_d(x_N) + \sum_{k=0}^{N-1} \left(L(x_k, u_k) - r^{\mathrm{T}} \sigma_k \right)$$

$$\text{subject to } x_{k+1} = f_d(x_k, u_k)$$

$$x_0 = x_\circ$$

$$G(x_k, u_k, \sigma_k) = 0$$

where:

$$G(x_k, u_k, \sigma_k) = \begin{bmatrix} g_1(x_k, u_k) \\ \vdots \\ g_{n_g}(x_k, u_k) \\ h_1(x_k, u_k) + \sigma_{1k}^2 \\ \vdots \\ h_{n_h}(x_k, u_k) + \sigma_{n_h k}^2 \end{bmatrix}$$

To solve an optimization problem with equality constraints, we can use Lagrange multipliers. The Lagrangian is defined as:

$$\mathcal{L}(x, u, \sigma, \lambda, \mu) = \phi_d(x_N, N) + (x_\circ - x_0)^{\mathrm{T}} \lambda_0$$

$$+ \sum_{k=0}^{N-1} \Big(L(x_k, u_k) - r^{\mathrm{T}} \sigma_k$$

$$+ (f_d(x_k, u_k) - x_{k+1})^{\mathrm{T}} \lambda_{k+1}$$

$$+ G(x_k, u_k, \sigma_k)^{\mathrm{T}} \mu_k \Big)$$

Necessary conditions for a point to be an extremum is the following partial derivatives to be zero:

$$\frac{\partial \mathcal{L}}{\partial x_k} = 0$$

$$\frac{\partial \mathcal{L}}{\partial \lambda_k} = 0 \qquad \qquad \text{for } k = 0, \ldots, N$$

$$\frac{\partial \mathcal{L}}{\partial \sigma_k} = 0$$

$$\frac{\partial \mathcal{L}}{\partial u_k} = 0$$

$$\frac{\partial \mathcal{L}}{\partial \mu_k} = 0 \qquad \qquad \text{for } k = 0, \ldots, N-1$$

The Lagrangian $\mathcal{L}$ can be rewritten as:

$$\mathcal{L}(x, u, \sigma, \lambda, \mu) = \phi_d(x_N) + x_\circ^T \lambda_0 - x_N^T \lambda_N$$
$$+ \sum_{k=0}^{N-1} \left(\mathcal{H}(x_k, u_k, \sigma_k, \lambda_{k+1}, \mu_k) - x_k^T \lambda_k \right)$$

where the Hamiltonian is defined as:

$$\mathcal{H}(x_k, u_k, \sigma_k, \lambda_{k+1}, \mu_k) = L(x_k, u_k) - r^T \sigma_k$$
$$+ f_d(x_k, u_k)^T \lambda_{k+1} + G(x_k, u_k, \sigma_k)^T \mu_k$$

Now, the optimality conditions can be summarized as in the following table. These conditions are known as Pontryagin's Maximum Principle.

Partial derivatives	Optimality conditions
$\frac{\partial \mathcal{L}}{\partial \lambda_{k+1}} = 0$	$x_{k+1}^\star = f_d(x_k^\star, u_k^\star)$
$\frac{\partial \mathcal{L}}{\partial \lambda_0} = 0$	$x_0^\star = x_\circ$
$\frac{\partial \mathcal{L}}{\partial x_k} = 0$	$\lambda_k^\star = \mathcal{H}_x(x_k^\star, u_k^\star, \sigma_k^\star, \lambda_{k+1}^\star, \mu_k^\star)$
$\frac{\partial \mathcal{L}}{\partial x_N} = 0$	$\lambda_N^\star = \frac{\partial}{\partial x_N} \phi_d(x_N^\star)$
$\frac{\partial \mathcal{L}}{\partial u_k} = 0$	$\mathcal{H}_u(x_k^\star, u_k^\star, \sigma_k^\star, \lambda_{k+1}^\star, \mu_k^\star) = 0$
$\frac{\partial \mathcal{L}}{\partial \sigma_k} = 0$	$\mathcal{H}_\sigma(x_k^\star, u_k^\star, \sigma_k^\star, \lambda_{k+1}^\star, \mu_k^\star) = 0$
$\frac{\partial \mathcal{L}}{\partial \mu_k} = 0$	$G(x_k^\star, u_k^\star, \sigma_k^\star) = 0$

For $k = 0, \ldots, N-1$ where $\star$ denotes the optimal solution and $\mathcal{H}_u = \frac{\partial \mathcal{H}}{\partial u_k}$ and $\mathcal{H}_\sigma = \frac{\partial \mathcal{H}}{\partial \sigma_k}$. In the next section, we introduce an algorithm to find a solution of the optimality conditions.

3.1 Continuation GMRES Method

Following [7], optimality conditions can be written as the equation $F(x_n, U) = 0$ where

$$F(x_n, U) = \begin{bmatrix} \mathcal{H}_u(x_0, u_0, \sigma_0, \lambda_1, \mu_0) \\ \mathcal{H}_\sigma(x_0, u_0, \sigma_0, \lambda_1, \mu_0) \\ G(x_0, u_0, \sigma_0) \\ \vdots \\ \mathcal{H}_u(x_{N-1}, u_{N-1}, \sigma_{N-1}, \lambda_N, \mu_{N-1}) \\ \mathcal{H}_\sigma(x_{N-1}, u_{N-1}, \sigma_{N-1}, \lambda_N, \mu_{N-1}) \\ G(x_{N-1}, u_{N-1}, \sigma_{N-1}) \end{bmatrix}$$

and:

$$U = [u_0^T, \ldots, u_{N-1}^T, \sigma_0^T, \ldots, \sigma_{N-1}^T, \mu_0^T, \ldots, \mu_{N-1}^T]^T$$

Dynamics equations of the states and costates (Lagrange multipliers corresponding to state equations) are given as:

$$x_{k+1} = f_d(x_k, u_k)$$
$$x_0 = x_n$$
$$\lambda_k = \mathcal{H}_x(x_k, u_k, \sigma_k, \lambda_{k+1}, \mu_k)$$
$$\lambda_N = \frac{\partial}{\partial x_N} \phi_d(x_N)$$

Using the *Continuation method*, instead of solving $F(x, U) = 0$, we find U such that:
$$\dot{F}(x, U) = A_s F(x, U)$$
where A_s is a matrix with negative eigenvalues. Now, we have:

$$F_x \dot{x} + F_U \dot{U} = A_s F(x, U)$$

To compute $\dot{U}$ using the following equation, which is linear in $\dot{U}$, we use the generalized minimum residual (*GMRES*) algorithm.

$$F_U \dot{U} = A_s F(x, U) - F_x f(x, u)$$

To compute U at any given time, we need to have an initial value for U and then use the above $\dot{U}$ to update it.

4   Example

In this section, we will apply the proposed workflow for MPC controller design to an Electro Hydraulic Servo System (EHSS). The EHSS system, depicted in Fig. 2, consists of mechanical system with two arms. The pressure inside a hydraulic cylinder creates the force to move the arms up and down. The model of this system is built in MapleSim by connecting components from Multibody and Hydraulics libraries (Fig. 3). The implementation of the EHSS model in MapleSim, generating code for the MPC controller in Maple and simulating the MPC controller in MapleSim are available upon request.

In a Maple worksheet, equations of motion of the EHSS system are extracted from the MapleSim model. For this example, the extracted equations represent an implicit ODE. In order to convert the equations into an explicit ODE, we will assume that the input of the system (the input pressure to the hydraulic circuit) and the derivative variables (state variables) are given. Then, we need to create a procedure to compute the derivatives of the state variables. In this particular case, the implicit ODE contains piecewise expressions that lead to a fairly complicated piecewise explicit ODE. To simplify the resulting ODE, a few of the expressions are approximated with rational polynomial functions.

Once the explicit ODE is computed, the MPC algorithm can be generated in Maple. One of the advantages of a symbolic computation engine such as Maple

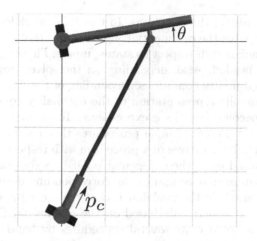

Fig. 2. EHSS system

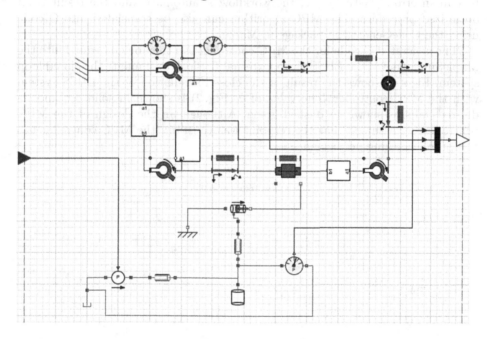

Fig. 3. EHSS MapleSim model

is that it can work on procedures as opposed to numbers. For example, by applying the codegen:-optimize command in Maple to a procedure, you can create a new procedure that computes the same result as the original procedure but it performs fewer operations. This optimization is done by recognizing common subexpressions that appear in the equations several times and computing them as intermediate variables. The intermediate variables are then only used, not recomputed, in the rest of the equations. In the MPC workflow, a procedure is generated that computes the optimality conditions. To that end, partial derivatives of the Hamiltonian with respect to states, inputs, Lagrange multipliers and slack variables are needed. Also, depending on the solver, we might need the derivatives of the optimality conditions. Depending of the dynamic equations of the system, the symbolic representation of the optimality conditions and their derivatives might become very long expressions. To avoid working with complicated expressions, we create Maple procedures that compute the optimality conditions. The partial derivatives of a procedure with respect to its input arguments can be computed using the codegen:-JACOBIAN command. The result is returned as a procedure that computes the corresponding derivative. The main advantage of using Maple in the workflow is that the procedures and their derivatives are computed automatically based on the original ODE equation. Users of numerical tools have to write several procedures by hand to implement an MPC controller. Manually writing procedures takes time and is always prone to human errors. With Maple, the workflow is automatic and the result is an optimized procedure. The MPC algorithm can also be translated into C code using the CodeGeneration package in Maple.

The generated C code for the MPC controller can then be embedded into the MapleSim model of the EHSS as an External C Block to simulate the closed loop system. Figure 4 shows the result of the closed simulation of the EHSS system with the MPC controller. The value of θ (Fig. 2) is shown in solid red and its desired value is shown in dashed green. Although, in the design of the MPC controller, we assumed that the setpoint was constant, the MPC controller has acceptable tracking performance.

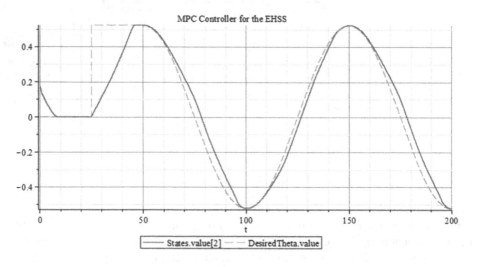

Fig. 4. Closed loop simulation

5   Summary

In this paper, we reviewed a workflow for implementing MPC controllers. MapleSim, a high-level modeling tool, and Maple, a high-level and symbolic computation engine, were employed to create an automatic workflow from a high-level model of the system to the C code of the MPC controller. The MPC problem formulation and solver were generated in Maple and then converted to C code. The main advantage of using a symbolic tool in the workflow is that the required procedures and their corresponding derivatives are computed and optimized automatically. This workflow saves time and it is less sensitive to human errors.

References

1. Maplesoft, a division of Waterloo Maple Inc.: MapleSim (2016)
2. Maplesoft, a division of Waterloo Maple Inc.: Maple (2016)
3. Qin, S.J., Badgwell, T.A.: A survey of industrial model predictive control technology. Control Eng. Pract. **11**, 733–764 (2003)
4. Qin S.J., Badgwell T.A.: An overview of nonlinear model predictive control applications. In: Allgöwer F., Zheng A. (eds.) Nonlinear Model Predictive Control. Progress in Systems and Control Theory. Springer, Switzerland (2000)
5. Boyd, S., Vandenberghe, L.: Convex Optimization. Cambridge University Press, Cambridge (2004)
6. Diehl, M., Ferreau, H.J., Haverbeke, N.: Efficient numerical methods for nonlinear MPC and moving horizon estimation. In: Magni, L., et al. (eds.) Nonlinear Model Predictive Control. LNCIS, vol. 384, pp. 391–417. Springer, Heidelberg (2009)
7. Ohtsuka, T.: A continuation/GMRES method for fast computation of nonlinear receding horizon control. Automatica **40**, 563–574 (2004)

Reduce the Complexity of the Polyhedron Minimization Using the Max Plus Pruning Method

Yassamine Seladji[✉]

STIC Laboratory, University of Tlemcen, Tlemcen, Algeria
yassamine.seladji@gmail.com

Abstract. The polyhedral analysis is widely used for the static analysis of programs, thanks to its expressiveness but it is also time consuming. To deal with that, a sub-polyhedral analysis has been developed which offers a good tread off between expressiveness and sufficiency. This analysis is based on a set of directions which is defined statically at the beginning of the analysis. More the cardinality of Δ is big, more the precision of the result is high. Even if the set Δ is big, the sub-polyhedral analysis can be done in a linear time. The bottleneck is that to construct the resulting polyhedron with a large number of constraints (one constraints per direction) is time consuming. In this article, we present a minimization method that allows to deal with that, using the max plus pruning method. We demonstrate the efficiency of our method on some benchmarks. The first results are very encouraging.

1 Introduction

In the abstract interpretation [2,3], the key component is represented by the abstract domain. A lot of them have been developed to deal with the multiple challenges of the program analysis. The most expressiveness one is the polyhedra abstract domain [4], but its analysis is time consuming. To deal with that, a lot of effort have been done by the researchers in the field and that to find a good trade-off between expressiveness and efficiency. A lot of domains have been developed, known as the sub-polyhedra or weakly relational abstract domains [6,8,9,11,12]. The authors in [10] present an abstract domain based on support functions, noted $\mathbb{P}^\sharp_\Delta$. This domain proposes a good balance between expressiveness and computational time. The lattice of $\mathbb{P}^\sharp_\Delta$ is closed to the lattice of the template abstract domain [9], but its result is more accurate than the one obtained using the template analysis. Because the precision of the polyhedral analysis is preserved using the $\mathbb{P}^\sharp_\Delta$ analysis and that based on the choice of a finite set of direction Δ. The larger the cardinality of Δ, the higher the precision of the result.

The execution time of the $\mathbb{P}^\sharp_\Delta$ analysis is linear in the cardinality of Δ. So, we can get a precise post fixed point using a large number of random directions. The problem is that taking a large number of directions means that the obtained

S. Bogomolov et al. (Eds.): NSV 2016, LNCS 10152, pp. 96–104, 2017.
DOI: 10.1007/978-3-319-54292-8_9

polyhedron contains the same number of constraints. So, the minimisation of this polyhedron is very time consuming. Because the minimization method, firstly, deletes the redundant constraints then computes the intersection of the other constraints. In this article, we present a new version of the polyhedral minimization method, called the k-minimization. This methods is based on the max plus pruning method [5].

2   Background

2.1   The Sub-polyhedral Abstract Domain Based Support Functions

The sub-polyhedral abstract domain presented in [10] is based on support function [7]. This domain is an abstraction of convex polyhedra over $\mathbb{R}^n$, where n is the space dimension. We denote by $\mathbb{P}^\sharp_\Delta$ the abstract domain using support functions. The lattice definition is closed to the lattice of the Template abstract domain [9]. $\mathbb{P}^\sharp_\Delta$ is parametrize by a finite set of directions $\Delta = \{d_1, \ldots, d_l\}$. The directions in Δ are uniformly distributed on the unit sphere, noted B^n. The definition of $\mathbb{P}^\sharp_\Delta$ is given as follow:

Let $\Delta \subseteq B^n$ be the set of directions. We define $\mathbb{P}^\sharp_\Delta$ as the set of all functions from Δ to $\mathbb{R}_\infty$, i.e. $\mathbb{P}^\sharp_\Delta = \Delta \to \mathbb{R}_\infty$. We denote $\bot_\Delta$ (resp. $\top_\Delta$) the function such that $\forall d \in \Delta$, $\bot_\Delta(d) = -\infty$ (resp. $\top_\Delta(d) = +\infty$).

For each $\Omega \in \mathbb{P}^\sharp_\Delta$, we write $\Omega(d)$ the value of Ω in direction $d \in \Delta$. Intuitively, Ω is a support function with finite domain.

The abstraction and concretization functions of $\mathbb{P}^\sharp_\Delta$ are defined as follows:

Let $\Delta \subseteq B^n$ be the set of directions.

We define the concretization function $\gamma_\Delta : \mathbb{P}^\sharp_\Delta \to \mathbb{P}$ by:

$$\forall \Omega \in \mathbb{P}^\sharp_\Delta, \ \gamma_\Delta(\Omega) = \bigcap_{d \in \Delta} \{x \in \mathbb{R}^n, <x, d> \le \Omega(d)\} \ .$$

where, $<x, d>$ is the scalar product of x by the direction d.

The abstraction function $\alpha_\Delta : \mathbb{P} \to \mathbb{P}^\sharp_\Delta$ is defined by:

$$\forall \mathsf{P} \in \mathbb{P}, \alpha_\Delta(\mathsf{P}) = \begin{cases} \bot & \text{if } \mathsf{P} = \emptyset \\ \top & \text{if } \mathsf{P} = \mathbb{R}^n \\ \lambda d. \ \delta_\mathsf{P}(d) & \text{otherwise} \end{cases} \ .$$

where, $\delta_\mathsf{P}(d)$ is the support function of the polyhedron P in the direction d, and $\mathbb{P}$ represents the polyhedra abstract domain.

Note that, the concretization of an abstract element of $\mathbb{P}^\sharp_\Delta$ is a polyhedron defined by the intersection of half-spaces, where each one is characterized by its normal vector $d \in \Delta$ and the coefficient $\Omega(d)$. The abstraction function on the other side is the restriction of the support function of the polyhedra on the set of directions Δ. The order structure of $\mathbb{P}^\sharp_\Delta$ is defined using properties of support functions [7]. The static analysis of a program consists in computing the least fixed point of a monotone map. To do so, the most used method is the Kleene

Algorithm. By combining the Kleene algorithm and the $\mathbb{P}^{\sharp}_{\Delta}$ abstract domain, the obtained algorithm has a polynomial complexity in the number of iterations and linear in the number of directions in Δ. In addition, its result is as accurate as possible: at each iterate, we have that $\Omega_i = \alpha_{\Delta}(\mathsf{P}_i)$, such that Ω_i (resp. P_i) is the result of the ith Kleene iteration using the $\mathbb{P}^{\sharp}_{\Delta}$ (respectively the polyhedra abstract domain). So $\Omega_{\infty} = \alpha_{\Delta}(\mathsf{P}_{\infty})$, with Ω_{∞} is the fixed point obtained in the $\mathbb{P}^{\sharp}_{\Delta}$ analysis and P_{∞} is the one obtained using polyhedra domain. That why the $\mathbb{P}^{\sharp}_{\Delta}$ analysis is more precise than the Template analysis [9]. In other terms, the $\mathbb{P}^{\sharp}_{\Delta}$ analysis is done with the precision of the polyhedra domain and the over-approximation is done only, at the end, in the concretization function. When with Template domain, all the analysis is done in a less expressive domain.

2.2   The Max Plus Pruning Method

In [5], the authors present a method to reduce the curse of dimensionality in solving an optimal control problem. In this method, the value function is over-approximated using a set of Max-Plus basis functions. The general formulation for the pruning problem appearing in max-plus basis methods is the following: Let $F = \{1, 2, \ldots, m\}$ be a set of integer, and let $g(x) : \mathbb{R}^n \mapsto \mathbb{R}$ be a function defined as follow:

$$g(x) = sup_{i \in F} g_i(x)$$

where $\forall i \in [1, m], g_i(x)$ is a basis function. Let $B = \{g_1, \ldots, g_m\}$ be the set of these m basis functions. Note that, when solving an optimal control problem the cardinality of B can be very large. The idea is to approximate $g(x)$ by keeping only $0 \leq k \leq m$ basis functions from the set B. For that, the authors in [5] need to compute the set $S \subset F$ with cardinality k and then approximate the function g by:

$$g(x) \simeq sup_{i \in S} g_i(x)$$

The obtained set S should minimize the approximation error. This is known as a pruning problem. To solve it, a set of witness points W is used to measure the approximation error, such that: $W = \{x_1, \ldots, x_m\} \subset \mathbb{R}^n$, where n is the space dimension. This set is constructed using a random points in the space. Afterwards, $\forall x_i \in W, \forall g_j \in B$ the importance metric is computed, which represents the distance between $g(x_i)$ and $g_j(x_i)$. This is denoted by c_{ij}, such that:

$$c_{ij} = g(x_i) - g_j(x_i)$$

The obtained results represents the cost matrix $C \in \mathbb{R}^m \times \mathbb{R}^m$ (dessiner la matrix). For a better comprehension, let us take the example of Fig. 1. In this example, we want to approximate the smooth convex function g (the red graph) using the basis functions g_0, g_1, g_2 (the green lines). The point x_0 is one witness point. It is used to compute the distance between the function g and all basis functions. The distance between $g(x_0)$ and $g_0(x_0)$ is represented by the red dashed line. In this example, if we want to keep only two of the three basis function. The couple (g_0, g_2) is the best choice.

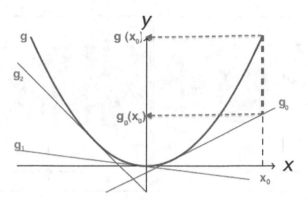

Fig. 1. In this figure, we represent the function g (red graph) and some basis functions (green lines). The dashed red line is the distance between g and g_0 using the point x_0. (Color figure online)

Afterwards, the cost matrix C is used to compute the set $|S| = k$. And that by applying one of the two methods:

– the K-median problem [1]: to minimize the sum of the lost, such that:

$$\min_{S \subset I} \sum_{i=1}^{m} \min_{j \in S} c_{ij}$$

– the K-center problem: to maximize the lost, such that:

$$\min_{S \subset I} \max_{i \in [1,m]} \min_{j \in S} c_{ij}$$

The obtained set S is used to approximate the function g as follow:

$$g(x) \simeq sup_{i \in S} g_i(x)$$

with $g_i \in B$.

3   The k-Minimization Method

In this section, we develop our main contribution which is a novel approach to reduce the complexity of the polyhedron construction and that by reducing the number of constraints, this method is called the *K-minimization*, which is inspired from the Max-Plus pruning method [5].

Let P^m be a polyhedron represented by the intersection of $m \in \mathbb{N}$ half-spaces i.e. $\mathsf{P}^m = \bigcap_{i=1}^{m} H_i$ where $H_i = \{x \in \mathbb{R}^n : \langle x, a_i \rangle \leq b_i\}$ with $a_i \in \mathbb{R}^n$ and $b_i \in \mathbb{R}$. For an m very large, the computation of P^m is time consuming. To improve this computation, we over-approximate P^m by keeping only $k < m$ of their half-spaces, let $\mathsf{P}^k = \bigcap_{i=1}^{k} H_i$ be the resulted polyhedron, such that:

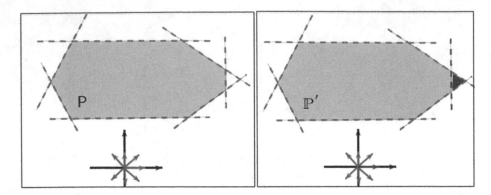

Fig. 2. (The left part) The intersection of the red dashed half spaces defines the poly-hedron P. The red directions in bottom represent the normal vectors of the lines those support these half-spaces. (The right part) the polyhedron P′ is an over-approximation of P, that by deleting the dashed blue half-space (Color figure online)

- $P^k \supseteq P^m$.
- P^k is the best approximation of P^m using k half-spaces. Note that, the definition of the best approximation strongly depend on the definition of the Hausdorff distance between two polyhedra.

For a better comprehension, let me explain the motivation using the example of Fig. 2. In this figure, the left polyhedron P is defined using the intersection of seven half-spaces. Each half space, is represented by one direction (given in red in the bottom of the left figure). We want to over-approximate P by taking only 6 half-spaces from the 7 one. The resulted polyhedron P′ is given in the right figure. Where, the half-space to delete is the blue dashed one. Noted that, P ⊆ P′, with P′ is the best approximation of P using only 6 half-spaces from the initial one. This approximation is known as the pruning problem, to be able to solve its automatically, we propose a method called the *K-minimization* method.

The *K-minimization* method is based essentially on three steps:

1 The computation of the witness points.
2 The computation of the cost matrix.
3 The application of the K-median algorithm.

Let us detailed these steps:

The witness points computation: Let $w \subseteq \mathbb{R}^n$ be a set of points, where each point of w belongs to one face of P^m. So, the cardinality of w is equal to m, *i.e.* $|w| = m$. In the following, each half-space H_i will be characterized by its corresponding point x_i in the set w, these points are called *witness points*. Note that, the computation of these points is known as a convex optimization problem and to solve it, we may solve m LP problems. For all $i \in \{1, \ldots, m\}$:

– Solve the following LP problem using the interior point algorithm:

$$\min \langle x, a_i \rangle - b_i$$

$$s.t. : \forall j \in \{1, \ldots, m\} \setminus \{i\}, \langle x, a_j \rangle \leq b_j$$

– Add the obtained point to w the witness point set.

The cost matrix computation. Let $C \in R^{m \times m}$ be a square matrix. We have that $\forall i, j \in [1, m]$ C_{ij} represents the euclidean distance between x_i the ith point in the set w and $proj(x_i, L_j)$ the orthogonal projection of x_i on the plane L_j. This distance is obtained as follows:

$$C_{ij} = \|x_i - proj(x_i, L_j)\|$$
$$= \frac{|\langle x_i, a_j \rangle - b_j|}{\|a_j\|}.$$

So, each line i of the matrix C contains distances between x_i and all the lines that support the faces of P^m. The matrix C is called *the cost matrix*.

The application of the k-median algorithm. To tackle the fact that we want to choose k half-spaces from the m ones and that by minimizing the approximation error, we propose the use of *the k-median algorithm* [1]. The k-median problem is one of the most studied clustering problem, such that for n points given in a metric space the aim is to identify the $k < n$ ones that minimize the sum of the distance to their nearest points.

In our problem, we want to define the k witness points such that the sum of the distance between these k points and their projections is minimized. For that, we use the cost matrix C to formalize the k-median problem as follows:

$$\min_{S \subset F, |S|=k} \sum_{i=1}^{m} \min_{j \in S} C_{ij}.$$

with $F = \{1, 2, \ldots, m\}$ the set of the witness point indices in w.

Several algorithms are known to solve this problem, and that returns the set S of indices of the witness points in w that minimize the sum of distance. We know that each witness point in w represents one half-space that is used to define P^m. So, the resulted polyhedron P^k is defined as follows:

$$\mathsf{P}^k = \bigcap_{i \in S} H_i.$$

Thus, we have that $\mathsf{P}^m \subseteq \mathsf{P}^k$.

To summarize, the k-minimization algorithm is given in Algorithm 1.

Algorithm 1. The K-minimization algorithm

Require: $\mathsf{P}^m, k \in \mathbb{N}$
 $w = witnessPoint(\mathsf{P}^n)$
 for $i = 0$ to $m - 1$ **do**
  for $j = 0$ to $m - 1$ **do**
   $C[i][j] = \text{Distance}(w[i], proj(w[i], L[j]))$
  end for
 end for
 $S = KmedianAlgo(C, k)$
 return P^k

In Algorithm 1, the set of witness points, noted w, is computed using the function $witnessPoint$. This function uses m LP solver. Then, the euclidean distance is computed between all the points of w and their orthogonal projection on L, where L are the set of planes that support the faces of the polyhedron P^m. These distances are computed using the function $Distance$ and the results are putted in the matrix C. Afterwards, the k-median algorithm is applied using the matrix C.

In the case of the $\mathbb{P}^{\sharp}_{\Delta}$ analysis, let Ω be the obtained fixed point. Then $\gamma_{\Delta}(\Omega) = \bigcap_{d \in \Delta} \{x \in \mathbb{R}^n, < x, d > \leq \Omega(d)\}$. This is the concretisation of Ω in the polyhedra abstract domain. Note that, the cardinality of Δ the set of directions can be very large, So the concretisation of Ω can be time consuming. That why, the $K\text{-}minimization$ method is applied at the end of the $\mathbb{P}^{\sharp}_{\Delta}$ analysis to over-approximate the result of $\gamma_{\Delta}(\Omega)$. The concretisation of Ω is very useful, it allows us to compare our result with the one obtained using the polyhedral analysis. It, also, can be used as the input of another analysis. Recall that the $\mathbb{P}^{\sharp}_{\Delta}$ analysis uses a polyhedron as initial input set. The preliminary results are given in the next section.

4   Benchmarks

We implemented the k-minimization algorithm on the top level of the Parma Polyhedra Library (PPL: http://bugseng.com/products/ppl/). We apply it on some programs, which represent digital filters. The obtained results are given in Fig. 3.

At the end of the $\mathbb{P}^{\sharp}_{\Delta}$ analysis, we concretise the result in the polyhedra abstract domain. In the table of Fig. 3, we compare the results obtained using the combination of the k-minimization and the $\mathbb{P}^{\sharp}_{\Delta}$ analysis [10], with the one obtained using only the $\mathbb{P}^{\sharp}_{\Delta}$ analysis. Note that, in the first result we apply the k-minimization method before the application of the concretisation function. Where in the second one, we apply the concretisation function directly on the result of the $\mathbb{P}^{\sharp}_{\Delta}$ analysis, and that using all the directions in Δ. The first results are very encouraging, with our method the analysis terminates in some minutes. Where with the standard minimization function the analysis did not terminates,

Program			The $\mathbb{P}_\Delta^\sharp$ analysis + the K-minimization		The $\mathbb{P}_\Delta^\sharp$ analysis
Name	$|V|$	$|\Delta|$	$t(s)$	K	$t(s)$
lead_leg_controller	5	350	$1m53.811s$	116	TO
lp_iir_9600_2	6	372	$3m0.165s$	124	TO
lp_iir_9600_4	10	500	$6m21.984s$	166	TO
lp_iir_9600_4_elliptic	10	500	$6m20.659s$	166	TO
lp_iir_9600_6_elliptic	14	692	$21m56.076s$	230	TO
bs_iir_9600_12000_10_chebyshev	22	1268	TO	422	TO

Fig. 3. The execution time obtained using the k-minimization method and the standard polyhedral minimization

and that after 10 h of executions. Even, with our method, the analysis of the last program did not terminate in a reasonable execution time. The lack of the k-minimization algorithm is the computation of the witness points which is time consuming, because we apply one LP solver per constraints. The improvement of this point is the subject of our ongoing work.

5   Conclusion

In the $\mathbb{P}_\Delta^\sharp$ analysis, The execution time is linear in the cardinality of Δ. So to improve the precision of the analysis, we can take Δ with a large cardinality. The result of this analysis can be concretised in the polyhedra abstract domain, where the number of the constraints of the obtained polyhedron is equal to the cardinality of Δ. So, if we take Δ very large, the computation of the resulted polyhedron can be time consuming. For that, we present in this paper a method called k-minimization. This method can be applied before the concretisation method to reduce its complexity. The k-minimization method is inspired from the Max-Plus Pruning method. This method over-approximate the obtained polyhedron by keeping only k from their half-spaces, where k is chosen statically smaller then the cardinality of Δ. The obtained over-approximation is the one that minimise the loss of precision.

References

1. Charikar, M., Guha, S., Tardos, É., Shmoys, D.B.: A constant-factor approximation algorithm for the k-median problem. In: Proceedings of the Thirty-First Annual ACM Symposium on Theory of Computing, pp. 1–10. ACM (1999)
2. Cousot, P., Cousot, R.: Abstract interpretation: a unified lattice model for static analysis of programs by construction or approximation of fixpoints. In: Conference Record of the Fourth ACM Symposium on Principles of Programming Languages (POPL 1977), pp. 238–252. ACM Press (1977)
3. Cousot, P., Cousot, R.: Comparing the Galois connection and widening/narrowing approaches to abstract interpretation. In: Bruynooghe, M., Wirsing, M. (eds.) PLILP 1992. LNCS, vol. 631, pp. 269–295. Springer, Heidelberg (1992). doi:10. 1007/3-540-55844-6_142

4. Cousot, P., Halbwachs, N.: Automatic discovery of linear restraints among variables of a program. In: POPL, pp. 84–97. ACM Press (1978)
5. Gaubert, S., McEneaney, W.M., Qu, Z.: Curse of dimensionality reduction in max-plus based approximation methods: theoretical estimates and improved pruning algorithms. In: CDC-ECE, pp. 1054–1061. IEEE (2011). http://dblp.uni-trier.de/db/conf/cdc/cdc2011.html#GaubertMQ11
6. Goubault, E., Putot, S., Védrine, F.: Modular static analysis with zonotopes. In: Miné, A., Schmidt, D. (eds.) SAS 2012. LNCS, vol. 7460, pp. 24–40. Springer, Heidelberg (2012). doi:10.1007/978-3-642-33125-1_5
7. Hiriart-Urrut, J.B., Lemaréchal, C.: Fundamentals of Convex Analysis. Springer, Heidelberg (2004)
8. Miné, A.: The octagon abstract domain. High. Order Symbolic Comput. 19(1), 31–100 (2006)
9. Sankaranarayanan, S., Sipma, H.B., Manna, Z.: Scalable analysis of linear systems using mathematical programming. In: Cousot, R. (ed.) VMCAI 2005. LNCS, vol. 3385, pp. 25–41. Springer, Heidelberg (2005). doi:10.1007/978-3-540-30579-8_2
10. Seladji, Y., Bouissou, O.: Numerical abstract domain using support functions. In: Brat, G., Rungta, N., Venet, A. (eds.) NFM 2013. LNCS, vol. 7871, pp. 155–169. Springer, Heidelberg (2013). doi:10.1007/978-3-642-38088-4_11
11. Simon, A., King, A., Howe, J.M.: Two variables per linear inequality as an abstract domain. In: Leuschel, M. (ed.) LOPSTR 2002. LNCS, vol. 2664, pp. 71–89. Springer, Heidelberg (2003). doi:10.1007/3-540-45013-0_7
12. Venet, A.J.: The gauge domain: scalable analysis of linear inequality invariants. In: Madhusudan, P., Seshia, S.A. (eds.) CAV 2012. LNCS, vol. 7358, pp. 139–154. Springer, Heidelberg (2012). doi:10.1007/978-3-642-31424-7_15

A Mode-Aware Contract Language for Reactive Systems

Cesare Tinelli[(✉)]

The University of Iowa, Iowa City, USA
cesare-tinelli@uiowa.edu

Abstract. Contract-based software development is a major methodology for the development of safety- and mission-critical embedded systems. Contracts are an effective mechanism to establish boundaries between components, and can be used efficiently to verify global, system-level properties by means of compositional reasoning techniques. A contract specifies the *assumptions* a component makes on its environment, and the *guarantees* it provides. Requirements in a component's specification are often case-based, with each case referring to a particular behavioral *mode* for the component. This talk introduces CoCoSpec, a mode-aware assume-guarantee-based contract language for embedded systems. CoCoSpec, which is built as an extension of the synchronous data-flow language Lustre, lets users specify mode behavior directly, thus preserving mode-specific information contained in (natural language) system requirements. Mode-aware model checkers supporting CoCoSpec can increase the effectiveness and scalability of compositional analysis techniques based on the assume-guarantee paradigm. In particular, they can leverage the fine-tunable abstraction mechanism provided by modes in order to selectively abstract complex numerical operations by their contracts, thus facilitating the verification of systems with numerical components. The talk presents the CoCoSpec language and illustrates the benefits of mode-aware model-checking on a case study involving a flight-critical avionics system. The evaluation uses Kind 2, a collaborative, parallel, SMT-based model checker developed at the University of Iowa that provides full support for CoCoSpec.

This work is was partially funded by NASA under Grant # NNX14AI09G.

S. Bogomolov et al. (Eds.): NSV 2016, LNCS 10152, p. 105, 2017.
DOI: 10.1007/978-3-319-54292-8

Author Index

Printed in the United States
By Bookmasters